NETLIVING 101
Networking Life's Journey

Networking Life's Journey
by

John C. Durkin

AuthorHouse™
1663 Liberty Drive
Bloomington, IN 47403
www.authorhouse.com
Phone: 1-800-839-8640

© 1999, 2000 by John C. Durkin. All rights reserved.

No part of this book may be reproduced, stored in a retrieval system, or transmitted by any means without the written permission of the author.

Published by AuthorHouse   02/04/2013

ISBN: 978-1-5872-1858-3 (sc)
ISBN: 978-1-4772-8034-8 (e)

Any people depicted in stock imagery provided by Thinkstock are models, and such images are being used for illustrative purposes only.
Certain stock imagery © Thinkstock.

This book is printed on acid-free paper.

Because of the dynamic nature of the Internet, any web addresses or links contained in this book may have changed since publication and may no longer be valid. The views expressed in this work are solely those of the author and do not necessarily reflect the views of the publisher, and the publisher hereby disclaims any responsibility for them.

About the Book

"It is not what you know, but who you know that counts." This old cliché is as true today as it was when it was first uttered. According to a recent survey conducted by Drake Beam Morin, Inc. (a large outplacement organization), networking fills 70 percent of professional positions. Networking for a job is the best way to tap into the unpublished job market. *NETLIVING 101, Networking Life's Journey* reaches beyond the job market into all aspects of life from the womb to the tomb. Hence the word *networking* is replaced by my newly coined word *netliving©*.

There is currently no book as indicated by reviewing *Books in Print* that shows people how to take advantage of networking techniques used in job hunting to enhance other facets of their lives. *NETLIVING 101, Networking Life's Journey* fills that gap by providing all the tools and information readers need to establish networks and have more enjoyable and successful lives. One of the reasons for choosing the title *NETLIVING 101, Networking Life's Journey* was because to the best of my knowledge no college or university offers a course as part of a curriculum on the subject.

In earlier, simpler times when most of the world's population lived in small villages where everyone knew their neighbor there was no need to build networks for they were already in place. The local church or pub was usually the hub of the network. With the complexity of today's society it has become necessary to make a concerted effort to establish support networks in order to be successful and happy.

In this self-help book; ideas, examples and suggestions for *netliving* are developed through short vignettes based on the lives of real people. Names and places will be changed to protect the innocent.

NETLIVING 101, Networking Life's Journey is written using the concept known as faction. Essentially, faction refers to the inclusion of certain details, which, although they may not have occurred exactly as described in point of fact, give the reader a clear image of the scene in his or her imagination. Rather than telling the reader what netliving is all about this book demonstrates through the words and actions of the characters. Chapter One introduces the two key characters that appear throughout the book. Roberta and Richard are used alternately, from chapter to chapter, to provide different perspectives. The fabric of friendships is woven through the stages of life and applied to various life experiences from overcoming the fear of public speaking to preparing for retirement.

Netliving 101, Networking Life's Journey is designed for individuals who are career oriented, sophisticated, and thoughtful. Most people are concerned about their future and are taking steps to afford themselves successful, happy and prosperous "mature years."

If your project is for a year, sow a seed.
If it is for ten years, plant a tree.
If a hundred, teach the people.

If you reap once only – it will be a one-
Time thing.
Planting a tree, it will be tenfold.
Teaching the people, the result is a
Hundred fold.

If you give a man a fish, he will be
Nourished once.
If you teach him to fish, he will feed
Himself and his family all his life.

Chuang Tzu, a Chinese
Taoist philosopher.
Written 26 centuries ago

ACKNOWLEDGMENTS

I would like to begin by thanking a longtime colleague, Dr. Mel Allerhand, who helped formulate my overall approach to this book. My wife, Peg, was a tremendous source of strength and wisdom. Besides sharing her good judgment, she read each chapter and did the initial editing. Nell & Ken Haughton of The Secretarial Shop added to the depth and clarity of the finished work. Artists Judy Risko and Kelli Swan helped with the illustrations and cover. Special thanks to Bob Janson and Rich Vacca for reviewing the manuscript and making strong suggestions. Finally my thanks to the many people interviewed who shared great netliving ideas.

JCD

DEDICATION

In memory of my parents:

John William & Mary Catherine Dempsey Durkin

INTRODUCTION

While serving as Chairman of the New Careers for Older Americans Committee (the function of which was to find positions for displaced older workers) in the early 1980s the idea to write a book outlining the keys to successful living dawned on me. In the Spring of 1983 with the help of a colleague, Dr. Mel Allerhand, a survey questionnaire was developed and distributed to a relatively small sample of what was considered "successful people."

One of the questions on the survey was: Did you feel you had a group of associates, family or friends (network) whom you could call on for support or in some cases did you use them as a sounding board for ideas? Could they be used in time of an emergency for help and resources? For example, if your hot water tank went out and you did not have the money to buy a new one, did you have a family member, friend or neighbor you could call and ask for help and/or advice?

It went on to state that Webster's New American Dictionary defines "network" as a *fabric* or structure of crossed threads, cords or wires. The networks covered in this question are made up of human beings who are similar to woven fabric in the frequency of transactions and interactions.

The response to that question was the genesis of my coining the word Netliving©. Netliving©, the concept of expanding the definition of networking to include all aspects of life, through all phases of life; hence replacing the word *working* with *living*.

This self-help book deals with the process of establishing support networks with others: from the womb to the tomb, in all aspects of life. The concept of "netliving" is explored as one of the secrets to successful living. NETLIVING 101, Networking Life's Journey offers thought provoking ideas, interesting examples and practical suggestions for "netliving." These are developed through brief vignettes based on the lives of real people.

Chapter One introduces the two key characters who appear throughout the book. Roberta and Richard are used alternately, from chapter to chapter, to provide different perspectives. As the fabric of friendships are woven through the stages of life and applied to various life experiences from overcoming the fear of public speaking to preparing for retirement.

The key to finding a job, especially during rough economic times is netliving. Some call it "interviewing for information" but it is making contacts and using these contacts to open doors for interviews, job offers and eventually employment. The old success story in the job market is " ...it isn't what you know, but who you know." National surveys conducted by Drake Beam Morin, Inc. (a large outplacement organization), show networking fills 70 percent of professional positions.

NETLIVING 101, Networking Life's Journey is designed for the 75 million "Baby Boomers" who are career oriented, sophisticated, thoughtful people. "Boomers" are concerned about their future and are taking steps to afford themselves successful, happy and prosperous "mature years."

According to a recent survey commissioned by Equitable Life Assurance Society of New York, Baby Boomers (born between 1946 and 1964) are saving more aggressively than ever. The majority of baby boomers (82%) are saving toward retirement, their children's education and their home according to the study conducted by Kane, Parson & Associates and it includes 600 baby boomers. Only a tiny portion (13%) believe they can depend on Social Security payments to support their retirement.

Personal financial planning and many other topics are covered in this book that will help the baby boomers as well as the following generations live fuller, more successful lives.

WHAT IS NETLIVING©?

Netliving is combining business, career and social networking. Effective networking is based on relationships that are cultivated and nurtured over a period of time so that mutual exchange of information, advice and support are shared. Netliving extends networking to all aspects of life beyond, but including the work world. Netliving extends its use from the bassinet to the internet. Netliving is a *journey* rather than a destination. Netliving is an on-going, proactive relationship-building *process;* planned connections with other human beings to facilitate accomplishing the job, reaching the goal or solving the problem.

Netliving looks to the future and is a long term strategy. Netliving works both ways. Netliving is finding out whom you want to get to know better and developing relationships that enhance your life and the life of your fellow networker. Netliving requires global thinking, strong written and oral communications. It requires skills in knowledge vehicles like the telephone, computer and internet. Netliving can be described as the art and science of the possible. . .

CONTENTS

Acknowledgments ix
Dedication... xi
Introduction xiii
What Is Netliving©?... xv
Contents xvii

Chapter One: From The Womb 1
Chapter Two: Through The Stages Of Life 13
Chapter Three: To The Art Of Public Speaking 27
Chapter Four: For A Mentor 39
Chapter Five: For Financial Success 47
Chapter Six: Career Secrets 55
Chapter Seven: Peoplehood Vs Priesthood 65
Chapter Eight: To Lifelong Learning 77
Chapter Nine: For Emotional Balance 91
Chapter Ten: The Mid-Life Crisis 101
Chapter Eleven: Second Careers 111
Chapter Twelve: To Volunteerism And Good Health 123
Chapter Thirteen: The Twelve-Step Programs 131
Chapter Fourteen: Recipe For Leisure 145
Chapter Fifteen: The Battle Of The Sexes 157
Chapter Sixteen: For Problem Solving 167
Chapter Seventeen: To Comprehend Diversity 175
Chapter Eighteen: To Understand The Languages Of Love... 185

Chapter Nineteen: To Obtain Peace Of Mind 193
Chapter Twenty: Pre-Retirement Planning 201
Chapter Twenty One: The Healing Power Of Laughter 213
Chapter Twenty Two: On The Internet 223
Chapter Twenty Three: To Wall Off History 231
Chapter Twenty Four: To The Tomb 243

ILLUSTRATIONS

Figure 2-1: New Life Planning Model 11
Figure 6-1: Sources Of Human Resources 54
Figure 8-1: Old Life Planning Model 75
Figure 8-2: New Life Planning Model 76
Figure 9-1: Boiling Soup Of Emotions 90

CHAPTER ONE

FROM THE WOMB

"Take good care of your future because that's where you're going to spend the rest of your life."

Charles F. Kettering (1876-1958)

Roberta and Richard had been in their mother's womb for about six months and they were enjoying the warm and snug feeling it gave them. As fraternal twins, they had their system of unspoken communication.

They speculated about the circumstances of the night of their conception, and Richard had his vision of what happened on the New Year's Eve: His father and mother had a few drinks to welcome the New Year; they grew mellow and became amorous and before long they were making love. "This caused those little wiggly sperm from our father to go swimming up through our mother's tubes," he said. "As it turned out, two of them landed and stuck to two of mom's eggs and there we were."

The twins were somewhat aware that in a few short months they would be entering a cold and hostile place called "the world." They often talked of their future and what they could expect from their parents and family. Roberta and Richard had become close friends in this confining environment. Roberta was larger than Richard by a few ounces and even at this point in their lives, appeared to be the more dominant of the two.

When Labor Day weekend arrived, the unborn twins' parents attended a picnic given by their father's employer. As luck would have it, their mom and dad were on the dance floor whirling to the sounds of "Roll Out The Barrel" when their mom's water broke. You guessed it, she went into "labor" on Labor Day.

As was predictable, Roberta was the first to arrive on the scene. Richard followed a few minutes later. This set up a pattern that continued throughout their lives. Roberta took the lead while Richard was content to follow.

Quickly the twins realized they had been born to two young, struggling parents, both of whom worked full-time jobs. John, their father operated a dry cleaning store for a national chain and Mary their mother worked behind the counter and kept the books. Their interaction with the extended family began immediately. Aunts, uncles and cousins were often present in their home. Mary and John had some strong concerns about having to place the twins in daycare. It was an unavoidable fact of life. The parents read a book on raising children that attempted to answer the question of what effect daycare would have on the children's emotional health?

So far, experts were unable to establish definitive answers to this question. Authoritative follow-up tests that were conducted on daycare children suggested that daycare in itself is not noticeably positive or negative in its overall impact on the child's emotional health. It was also suggested that the parents should plan to arrange their schedule so that the four of them would have especially close, joyful and dependable periods of time together-- quality time.

John and Mary Dolan scheduled their activities around the twins waking hours and made sure their activities were of a quality level that would enhance their learning. They also read that they should give their children many opportunities to interact with other people, including adults as well as children.

Researchers found that children who attended preschool educational programs seemed to have better social skills than those who did not. In fact, some experts felt the sheer interactivity among children, their peers, and their adult teachers that was built into these programs fueled a great deal of the learning that occurred.

In addition, the twins' parents had set up regular time for them to play with other children. They encouraged their friends and relatives to spend quality time with them.. This eventually led to the formation of a "street center" by John and Mary Dolan along with several other parents in the neighborhood.

A street center was a program that provided parent education and support for families with newborns to five-year-olds. In these home-style preschool play groups, the parents rotated being playgroup hosts for the children from all the families. One helper parent assisted the host, and the rest of the parents had the time off. The twins enjoyed being with the large group of children from the beginning. Roberta, the born leader, would organize games such as "Hot Beans for Supper" with the other children and Richard would follow her lead along with the other children. In the game, Roberta would hide an object and yell "Hot Beans for Supper" when one of the children would get close to the hidden target. Their parents felt the center was a great idea for convenience and financial reasons.

The Dolan's backyard became a "sharing circle" eventually. A sharing circle was an efficient tool for collecting high-quality options for solving a specific problem. The leader invited the participants to sit in a circle and asked a person in the group to share a problem. It took three to five minutes to collect ideas from a dozen people. John Dolan recorded the suggestions made so the person with the problem had a written reminder to take home. Since the twins were their first children these "gems of wisdom" were welcomed by their parents. This helped to supplement their "Dr. Spock" guidelines.

There was a downside to these gatherings of children in one confined area. The cold and flu season came around and invariably one of the children would bring the latest bug along and with the sharing of toys and the thumb sucking (they were not particularly careful of whose they sucked) caused the spread of these germs and the ensuing time to recover. This was a small negative for all the positive benefits received in the opinion of the parents.

John Dolan fondly remembered his own childhood and the many great experiences he had had as a Boy Scout. He had learned many skills while earning merit badges. As a Cub Scout his pack was made up of nine and ten-year olds from his neighborhood. Then, when he was twelve, his group graduated to Scout Troop 411, which was affiliated with his family's church. His first scoutmaster was an ex-marine who had served in the Pacific theater during World War II. As the group gathered around the campfire, Mr. Martin told them war stories. The young boys loved the one about his landing on Iwo Jima and being present when the famous flag raising ceremony took place on Mt. Suribachi. Richard and Roberta would sit in rapture as their father told them about his many escapades while wearing a scout uniform.

The story they wanted to hear over and over again was "The Green Man" story. John Dolan had a knack for telling stories that he inherited from his father before him. It came from his Celtic origins, he would say. Getting back to the Green Man. He would begin by saying, "Once upon a time in the hills of Western Pennsylvania there lived a young man and his widowed mother." This young man was called Joe Young and was a tall, lanky handsome and kind youngster. He was a good son to his mother doing all the chores and working hard at his schoolwork. Everyone in the neighborhood liked him and always gave him a big smile when he waved at them on his way to and from school. Many native Pennsylvanians were wavers. It was a custom, especially in the rural sections; a sign of friendship and caring.

Young Joe was also a Boy Scout and one of the charter members of Troop 411. He took his scouting seriously and was always prepared. As he was walking home from school one fall afternoon he heard a loud scream, "HELP," "HELP," "PLEASE, SOMEONE, HELP ME DOWN." As Joe rounded the bend in the road he saw a young panic-stricken child of about age six stuck up in a telephone pole.

Apparently little Jimmy had been flying his kite in the nice autumn wind and had let it get up too high and it became snagged in the high voltage wires. Joe yelled to him, "HOLD ON, DON'T MOVE." With that Joe bounded up the pole thinking of nothing but saving this youngster. On the way up he was able to negotiate the network of wires and free the six year old. He brought him down and as an added gesture went back up to free the kite so the child would have it to play with the next day.

On the second trip Joe became entangled in the high voltage wires and was thrown from the pole. He sustained tremendous electrical burns. He had been hit across the face with one of the heavy voltage cables and it burned his nose completely off. It left two holes where his eyes once were and ripped off his left arm. When the ambulance arrived the EMS attendants had never seen such an accident where the victim was still alive. They rushed him to Rochester Hospital and worked for hours over him to save his life. They were successful but what they observed when the bandages were finally removed was difficult to look at and seemed almost inhuman.

The green from the copper wires left large marks on Joe's face and hence his new name became "The green man". He was so ugly his mother kept him in the basement during the day so he would not scare the children as they played. In the evening she would let him out and he would jog along the country roads. When John Dolan was older and could drive a car, he and his high school friends would take their dates out to see Joe and bring him some "Rolling Rock" which was his favorite beer. They got to know him and would carry on a conversation while he grunted approval. The dates would be aghast at the sight of Joe but once they got used to him he was an okay guy. He lived many years like this and when his mother died he was institutionalized. At this point in time he has probably passed to a better life.

Their father continued on to describe how he learned to safely use various woodworking machines such as lathes, drills, saber and circulars saws. He also learned how to defend himself. The ex-marine scoutmaster insisted they all learn to box. This was of great interest to young John Dolan since his father was a prizefighter and had already taught him the fundamentals of self-defense. As time moved along, their father had advanced to the Explorer Scout level and became involved in adult activities. The netliving he experienced with other boys and men in the scouting program prepared him to deal with similar situations later in life.

There was one experience John Dolan had in the Boy Scouts while camping that was not positive. He told this story to the twins because he felt they should hear about the "bitter as well as the sweet." They were camping at one of Mr. Martin's friend's camp one summer weekend having a ball. The cabin was located next to a slow moving river and the boys were enjoying swinging from a tire-swing into the water. After a day of hiking and swimming they were exhausted as they sat around the campfire telling scary stories about the "headless horseman" and the "wicked witch of the north."

The significant part of this story began when the lights went out in the cabin. The host turned out to be a pedophile who liked to caress young boys. Their father heard a commotion in the next bunk as one of his fellow scouts was punching the groping adult, and yelling, "Keep your filthy hands off me." Of course at that time they never had heard the term "sexual harassment." Mr. Martin was notified and that was the last time they ever camped at "Handy Andy's place" as it became known.

Mary Dolan, Roberta's mother, after hearing all this talk about the Boy Scouts, decided to have Roberta join the Girl Scout Brownies. She and Roberta attended meetings at the den mother's home and earned merit badges for sewing, cooking and service-oriented skills. In addition to the usual camping, swimming and water safety skills, Roberta received detailed training in the art of baby-sitting. She learned how to hold and feed an infant, and how to change and clean a young child. The classes taught the young ladies the proper emergency steps to take in the event a child swallowed a foreign object. They were taught to make sure they had a phone number to contact the parents or another responsible adult in case an emergency arose.

In the craft classes, the Girl Scouts (for now Roberta at twelve had advanced to that level) learned how to make favors for local hospital patients and nursing home residents. They were taught the proper approach to take with these afflicted individuals. These experiences helped Roberta to deal with afflicted loved-ones later in life.

The Girl Scout program taught its members to handle children's programs in the elementary schools. The scouts would entertain the first and second graders during recess periods. The interaction among the girls, the leader, Mrs. White and other mothers was helpful in stimulating Roberta's personality growth.

When some of Roberta's high school friends decided to become Candy Stripers (volunteers) at the local hospital, she decided to join them. Without thinking about her aversion to being in direct contact with sick people, she followed her friends. She did not like to see or even hear anything about blood; when she had to give blood for a routine physical it was a major issue. She always looked the other way as the nurse pricked her finger.

The thought that she would have to come face to face with people who might be bleeding or have worse conditions was more than Roberta was prepared to handle. When she told the hospital volunteer coordinating person about her problem, Roberta was immediately re-assigned to duty in the coffee shop. Thus, she avoided being exposed to sick or dying people.

As John Dolan became more involved in his dry cleaning business he joined the local chamber of commerce to netlive with its members. While attending a chamber meeting one evening he met another young father and they shared their concerns about business problems and personal problems. The subject of quality time with the family came up and Richard's father indicated he had not been spending enough time with his children especially his son who needed a male influence. Most of the teachers in school were female and he was home with a mother and sister. Feeling guilty about the time spent away from the family, he began to look for quality experiences he could share with his son. One day Richard came home from elementary school with a flyer describing the YMCA's Indian Guide Program for fathers and sons. The concept came in response to a need of so many busy fathers. This organization used the fathers' limited free time to provide quality experiences. Each group was known as a tribe; Richard and his father joined a tribe called the Iroquois. Richard was known in the tribe as "Running Deer," and his father's Indian name was "Walking Deer." They were taught that Indians gave action-oriented names to their people.

This was a joyful time for both Richard and John Dolan. They attended weekly meetings and performed challenging projects. It was a good opportunity for both of them to netlive with the other fathers and sons in the tribe. The most appealing feature of the Indian Guide program to Richard was he had his father "captured" for at least a few hours a week. They learned many new and fascinating skills. Both discovered how much they loved the great outdoors. More accurately Richard discovered and John re-discovered their love of nature. They went on camping trips during the spring, summer and fall. Richard found he was a natural horseman during their first trip to a six-hundred acre ranch for a horseback riding weekend. They learned all the safety precautions in a fenced-in corral. When they satisfied the riding instructor, they graduated to the open trails.

Richard enjoyed the experience so much that father and son returned to the ranch many times in the ensuing years. When he was twelve, Richard went to summer camp for a month, to his beloved Rolling-Y Ranch. The next year he worked as a junior counselor for the entire summer. The following year he became a full-blown camp counselor, and by then had became an excellent horseman.

Richard returned home every Labor Day weekend with many funny stories of happenings on the ranch during the summer. One summer his cousin from New York came and spent two weeks at the ranch and Richard was his counselor. His cousin was incensed when he found he would have to clean out the stables and curry comb the horses. He complained to Richard, "My father paid all those big bucks and you want me to do all this grunt labor?" "No way" he said in as firm a voice as he could. When his counselor explained to him that there would be no riding or eating until the chores were taken care of he began to see the light. He finally grunted that "No one ever told me that being a cowboy was such hard work."

During this time period Richard's father also gained from the Indian Guide experience. Besides the quality experiences he and Richard shared, he made some great contacts -- netliving in action. One night while the fathers from the Iroquois tribe were sitting on the bunk house porch they noticed some illegal activity going on in a cabin down the hill from them.

It seemed that some enterprising fathers had bought a case of Budweiser in the local town and had placed the bottles carefully in a spring-fed stream running behind their cabin. John Dolan and Jack Murphy another father from the tribe witnessed this activity and came up with a plan. Since it was against the ranch's regulations to have any alcoholic beverages on the premises, fathers Jack and John decided to help themselves to this liquid libation knowing that the owners could not make a fuss about it since they were in the wrong by bringing it onboard.

They sat on the porch enjoying their contraband and watching the other fathers scurrying around trying to find their missing beer. This created a bond between the two dads that lasted for many years. In fact, Richard's father was instrumental in finding employment for Jack Murphy with his own dry cleaning organization. This netliving experience enhanced their relationship. They shared a wide variety of life's activities together long after the boys graduated from the Indian Guide program and the YMCA's senior group known as "Trail Blazers."

From time to time Roberta and Richard experienced some sibling rivalry that was a challenge for their parents. But on the whole they were fond of each other and beware of anyone who tried to pick on either of them. The saying, "Blood is thicker than water" was true when it came to these twins.

John and Mary Dolan found that the growth of their children's personalities reached into other personalities. The detailed make-up of their characters depended upon the interpersonal relationships they experienced from day to day, age group to age group. The personalities were made up of attitudes, predisposition and potentialities, a complex pattern which took form within countless interpersonal relationships. These relationships were highly diversified. They included interpersonal forces which impinged upon the child at home, at school and in the community.

NETLIVING NOTES:

* Netliving will enhance your child's ability to learn and grow mentally. I've learned that you should never tell a child his/her dreams are unlikely or outlandish. Few things are more humiliating and what a tragedy it would be if he/she believed it.
* Netliving will improve your child's overall personality development. I've learned that your family won't always be there for you. It may seem funny, but people you aren't related to can take care of you and love and teach you to trust people again. Families aren't always biological.
* Netliving will help your childcare budget. I've learned that it's not what you have in your life but whom you have in your life that counts.

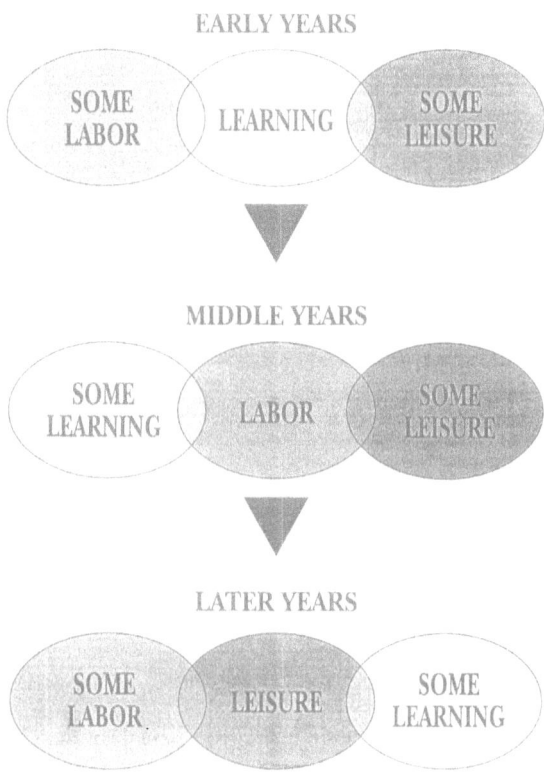

Figure 2-1

CHAPTER TWO

THROUGH THE STAGES OF LIFE

"A prudent man should always follow in the path trodden by great men and imitate those who are most excellent."

Niccolo Machiavelli (1469-1527)

Following the guidance provided by Dr. Spock's handbook, Roberta and Richard's parents watched for the patterns of behavior that were forecast from the "terrible twos" to the "noisy nines." They reflected on the life experiences that prompted them to make decisions which had a positive or negative effect on the rest of their lives.

These reflections on the Dolan's lives and the lives of other family members and friends indicated that developmental crises experienced during various stages of life helped individuals attain success or suffer failures. They knew that taking the proper steps when these developmental crises arose during the young person's stages of life meant either a pattern of successful living or one of destructive behavior.

At the age of ten, Richard purchased a daily newspaper route consisting of ten customers. The investment was ten dollars. Netliving this customer base, he additionally developed lawn mowing and baby-sitting opportunities. The local country club's caddymaster lived on Richards newspaper route, and he assisted by providing leads for choice weekend work assignments.

Richard, through netliving and shrewd negotiation, built his route of ten customers to the largest route in town, peaking at an impressive four hundred subscribers. All this was accomplished by the time Richard reached his sixteenth year.

There were some trying times along the way. On those cold winter evenings when he had to plow through mounds of snow to deliver the paper to the side door that had not been shoveled. The ice storm that knocked down the power lines and shot sparks everywhere he tried to walk on his route. Sometimes customers would skip town without paying their two or three week-old bills. Of course Richard had to absorb these losses since he was an independent contractor.

One of the worst experiences Richard had as a young paperboy took place the Friday night before Christmas one year. Three older boys were lying in wait for him as he returned home from collecting his money. They knew his pockets would be stuffed with bills and coins, especially when it was Christmas and the season's tips were also included. As they attacked him Richard remembered all the fighting techniques his dad had learned from Mr. Martin his ex-marine scout master. He held off the bullies by kicking and punching each one as they circled him for final thrust. Richard let out a loud Indian Guide war-cry and a neighbor came to help him. Mary, Roberta and especially John Dolan sat around the dinner table that night proud of their son and brother for standing up for himself and not cowering to those punks.

By the age of sixteen, Richard had convinced his parents that he needed a car. It had been a hard sell because his mother and father had concerns about his losing focus on his school work. Then what about Roberta? If Richard was permitted to own an auto why not her? After many long discussions they finally agreed, under the condition that if his school grades went down, the automobile went bye-bye. He also agreed to help his sister learn to drive and make the car available to her at least once a week.

Like most young men his age, Richard was in love with his car, a 1940 dark green Chrysler sedan. He washed and waxed it every weekend and tried to keep it in top running condition. His need for advanced mechanical knowledge caused him to form a network with some boys who worked at the local gas station; they knew plenty about repair and maintenance. This arrangement worked out well for the smooth running of "the tank" as Richard's friends called his beloved car. However, his parents were not impressed with his newfound friends. One of the boys, Rubin had come from West Virginia to work in his uncle's automobile dealership. This young man was the most knowledgeable of the group. The other two youths were local high school drop-outs.

Richard got along well with all of them, but had a special relationship with Rubin. He taught Richard how to sing country songs and they spent many hours cruising the roads and singing the night away.

On one of these evenings, the two local boys planned to break into a junk yard to steal some auto parts they needed. As they drove around, they explained their plan to Richard and "the hillbilly," as Rubin became known.

A signal went off in Richard's brain, telling him that this was one of those developmental crisis experiences about which his parents had told him. He firmly nudged his friend Rubin and explained he had to be home in a few minutes. His "hillbilly" friend picked up Richard's hint and quickly bailed out of the scheme.

The next afternoon while delivering his papers, Richard heard about the boys having been chased by a junkyard dog and then caught by law enforcement personnel and arrested. This incident unfortunately led to their being put on probation; they subsequently experienced many such brushes with the law, resulting in ever increasing consequences.

Richard, like many other young people during the fifties and sixties, joined the U.S. Navy after completing high school. It was the thing to do. He was eighteen years old. At the time of his enlistment, the Korean War was being waged between the North and South Koreans. The U.S. was an ally of the latter. Richard chose the U.S. Navy partly due to his family's traditional love of the sea, but the more practical reason for the choice was his total disinterest in being a foot soldier. The thought of being in a foxhole or sleeping in a tent surrounded by mud held no appeal for Richard.

On the positive side, the navy offered three sturdy meals a day, a clean bunk and an opportunity to learn a technical field (e.g., electronics.) In addition, the military was still offering an attractive G.I. Bill of Rights (a carry-over from World War II) that would help pay for his college education and the down payment on his first home when the time came.

Richard soon found himself far away from home without the moral or social support he had grown to expect. When his shipmates wanted to go out drinking and chasing women at the sailors' bars, Richard recognized the dilemma. He knew this could lead to getting drunk and possibly having sex with one of the "barflies." Richard decided to go along because he felt he needed the experience and he was tired of working so hard and having no fun . . . and the lure of wanting to be "one of the guys" was powerful.

He and his shipmates approached the Red Rooster, one of the infamous "gin mills" on the waterfront. Richard had developed into a leader and the other crew members looked up to him. He walked into the bar as if he owned the place and ordered. On the next bar stool sat an attractive older woman. She noticed the young men and asked if they wanted to see her tattoo. Richard stepped forward and said he would like to see it. She said, "It will cost you a beer." He slapped a five dollar bill on the bar and she lifted up her skirt to reveal she was without underpants. She gave a big howl and all the salty bar patrons went wild with glee.

Richard had been initiated into the ritual of the Rooster. He blushed a deep cherry red as it dawned on him what she had meant by her "tattoo." The rest of the evening was spent joking with other barmaids and sailors. Fortunately, he returned to his ship that night without any further incidents.

Richard kept a level head and did not go off the deep end with his newfound freedom. He remembered what his parents and other family members had told him when he enlisted in the navy, particularly his uncle Pat's warning to never get a tattoo.

Several months after the Red Rooster incident he and some of the other crew members were drinking quite heavily and feeling the effects of the alcohol. They got into a bit of a row with some Marines and it looked as if they would all spend the night in the brig. Fortunately the SP's were goodhearted guys. They let them go with the understanding they would return to the ship immediately.

Instead they climbed the front steps of a tattoo parlor. The young sailors kept egging each other on to get a tattoo. Richard, being the leader of the pack, was first in line. Just as his hand wrapped around the door knob of the tattoo parlor, his uncle's words came to him loud and clear, "Richard, whatever you do, don't get a tattoo. You will regret it 'til your dying day." Richard stopped dead in his tracks and retreated to the safety of his ship.

Years later Richard would encounter one of his less fortunate shipmates who went ahead and had a "dancing lady" tattooed on his right forearm that evening. He spent many painful hours having it removed and the resulting scar was unsightly.

The close call with the tattoo parlor was a defining moment in Richard's life. He felt like a new person the next day and decided to stay away from drinking and concentrate on his career as a high speed radio operator. For the rest of his time in the navy he worked hard at being the best radioman he could be. He studied the correspondence courses every opportunity he had spare time. When the test came up for his third class petty officer rating, he took it and passed with flying colors. The same was true for his second class rating, and then the coveted first class rating. All the time he was netliving with the more senior radiomen aboard the ship. He dogged them night and day and asked them so many "what if" questions it almost drove them around the bend.

Sadly, one of Richard's shipmates from boot camp went the other direction. He was influenced by the wrong group of sailors and ended up in the brig. This pattern of behavior continued, and after several periods in the brig, he received a dishonorable discharge. His ill-advised decisions brought negative results. It could have been such for Richard, except for the early positive netliving influences on Richard's life.

With his promotions and success in the navy, Richard learned to balance his life more. He had a tendency to be a workaholic so he made sure he took his liberty time when the ship was in port. He took every occasion to visit his sister Roberta when he was on the east coast. She was in college in the Washington D.C. area and they enjoyed getting together on weekends and touring the nation's capital. Although they were many miles apart most of the time when they were together it was as if they had never been apart. Richard would ask how mom and pop were doing and the extended family because Roberta was in closer touch with them and had more opportunity to return home for visits.

While at sea he learned to pleasure read. He read everything he could get his hands on in the ship's library. He came in contact with the ship's officers as a radioman and netlived with them on the subject of choosing a college when his enlistment was completed. They were helpful and supportive in this area.

In the last year of his enlistment, Richard found himself in charge of a radio shack on an ammunition ship. When he came aboard, the ship was docked at the navy yard undergoing a major overhaul. Therefore, he had the opportunity to netlive with the rest of the crew, especially the "radio gang." They spent hours drilling various emergency exercises since there wasn't much radio traffic while in dry dock.

Richard had less than a year to serve on his enlistment and four years of college beckoned on the horizon. He was excited about the future and also the prospect of taking the USS Mauna Loa on a shake-down cruise in the Atlantic the following week. Extensive work had been done on the engines and the time had come to test the ship at full speed.

Monday morning arrived and all hands prepared to weigh anchor. The radio crew were assembled in the radio shack to make sure all the circuits and frequencies were set. Richard was checking every transmitter to make sure they were putting out the proper amount of power. The ship was anchored in Gravesend Bay, adjacent to Coney Island. The deck crew quickly hoisted the anchor and got the large gray hulk moving despite its full load of ammunition. The capacity for this ship's holds was five thousand tons of bombs and explosives.

Once the harbor was cleared, the mustang captain of the USS Mauna Loa, AE-8, gave the order to test the engines at full throttle. The engine room was given the order to make turns for full speed ahead. Full speed on this World War II vintage war bucket was about fifteen knots. The old ship began creaking and moaning under the immense physical stress.

Then all hell broke loose. General Quarters sounded with its attention commanding repetitious gong, and added to that alarm were the feared words, "FIRE! FIRE IN THE STACK! THIS IS NOT A DRILL - REPEAT - THIS IS NOT A DRILL!" All at once everyone began rushing in various directions to get to the GQ stations.

Richard was in the radio shack, his general quarters station, where he set up new frequencies with the New York City Fire Department to request assistance since the ship was still within the continental limits and in the jurisdiction the NYCFD. He dashed back to the transmitter locker on the aft end of the ship. As he spun around the corner of the bulkhead he stopped short just as a fire crewman turned a four inch hose in the direction of the transmitter room. Richard yelled, "STOP! STOP! DON'T TURN THAT F-------HOSE ON!"

Fortunately Richard was able to stop the firemen in time, remembering that saltwater conducted electricity well and the sailors on the hose would have received a severe shock. He dialed the frequency into the big transmitter and established radio contact with the New York City Fire Department.

Meanwhile, two chief petty officers were climbing up the side of the burning stack with CO2 fire extinguishers trying to bring the blaze under control. It was determined that the engine exhaust rings were installed backwards, causing raw fuel oil to spray up the fiery hot exhaust stack.

The big concern aboard the Mauna Loa was that the fire would back up into the engine room and migrate to the ammunition holds. That concern was written on the face of every member of the crew including the seasoned mustang captain. There was no place to run. Richard and his shipmates knew that even if they jumped overboard there was no assurance of safety. If the ammo exploded, the concussion would crush anything in the water for miles around.

The only solution was to stay put and fight. Fight is what that valiant crew did for four long hours on the hot July day. Firefighters from the New York City Fire Battalion trained their huge hoses on the Mauna Loa, which helped keep the ammunition storage areas cool. The real heroes were two chief petty officers who used fifty-five fire extinguishers before the last flame was finally conquered. The event was even more exciting because the TV station helicopters broadcast the fire on the evening news and the story made the front page of the New York Times the following day.

Netliving and the resulting teamwork performed by a well-trained group saved the day when the U.S.S. Mauna Loa became and "active volcano."

As Richard moved through his final months in the navy he tried to keep his life in balance. He had a great time visiting all the many landmarks in the New York City area. At the same time he was preparing for his college entrance exams and studying math and science books that he had not touched in four years.

He was conscious that his main goal while in college was to master the tools that would earn him and his future family more than just a livelihood. He was also aware there was much more to college life than just "cracking the books." With the launching of "Sputnik" by the Russians many young people turned their attention to science as a career. Richard was one of them and decided to pursue a course in physics.

The university he chose to attend had a small but highly regarded physics department. This suited Richard fine since he was rusty on his math and science and the small classes gave him the opportunity to form a study network with other classmates and some of the professors. It was a struggle for him for the first semester and he felt more than once that he was going to flunk out.

Besides his sister, Roberta, Richard had established a substantial network of friends with a wide variety of interests and backgrounds. His job opportunities while attending the university gave him access to many wonderful people. One of his employers was close friends with a couple who had a daughter who needed to be taught to drive so she could help with the family chores. They enlisted Richard's services to be her driving instructor. This decision was made without consulting her and this was not well received by the potential driving student.

Richard's first encounter with Patty was not a pleasant one. He immediately came to the conclusion she was a spoiled brat and she in turn thought he was an old man. As a matter of fact he was five years older but because of his years in the navy the age difference was significant.

Gradually the relationship changed and they fell in love. They were always together for about two years, but they were constantly having arguments and disagreements. Finally they became engaged and the stress level increased. After a few months of this high tension they both decided they had had enough of this turmoil and went their separate ways.

Upon graduation from college, Richard decided to pursue a career in the corporate world that would enable him to make a good living for himself and his future family. In addition, he wanted a career that would not force him to become a workaholic. He planned to have the balanced life that he had learned about in college. He wanted to carry this mode of operating over into his life's work.

Richard had seen imbalance in the lives of his parents. Although they had made a conscious effort to keep their lives in balance, they had spent many hours in the dry cleaning business that could have been shared with his sister and himself in more pleasant pursuits.

Two years after Richard had begun his business career and his ex-fiancee had started her teaching career back home on Long Island, the tragic death of his cousin caused him to call Patty to let her know since they had double dated with this cousin. She was so upset by the news that she flew out to console Richard and within three months they were married.

Patty worked as a full-time teacher at a local all-girls high school and eighteen months later the first child arrived. Richard was excited about becoming a father and it motivated him to work harder and become more successful so his wife and his new son would be proud of him.

Richard chose human recourses management as a career. He utilized netliving to fill job openings and obtain other critical benchmark data. He developed and chaired the "Alumni Career Network" at his alma mater. Richard also chaired "New Careers for Older Americans." This organization's function was to find positions for displaced workers, the older group, using the netliving approach.

While in his early thirties, Richard became the father of another son and daughter to balance out the family. Patty had become a full time mother and took care of the home, joined the PTA and kept things running smoothly while Richard was on the road eighty percent of the time.

In reviewing the New Life Planning Model (See Figure 2-1), Richard felt he was on track. He was spending eighty percent of his time in the "labor" oval, and he balanced the other twenty percent of his time between "learning" and "leisure." Patty did not necessarily agree with this distribution of his time. She felt he was on the road too much and after five years of discussing it with her and his boss, Richard resigned his position after obtaining a better position with less travel through netliving his business network.

Like many of his friends, when Richard reached his mid forties, he experienced a mid-life crisis. He began to measure his time on earth not "from birth" but from, "how much time do I have left?" He did not go off the deep end and start chasing younger women as some of his friends had done, but he did begin to ask himself questions about the degree of success he had achieved. He began to netlive with other individuals who had gone through the same experience, and he began taking positive steps to overcome this apparent crisis.

He consulted with his sister and she was not experiencing the same crisis. It may have been a male thing or his twin was not in the same place as he was emotionally.

First, he began to get himself in better physical shape. He enrolled in a beginning tennis class at the local high school. In fact, Patty joined him in this endeavor but did not like tennis at all. He had never played tennis before and found, much to his delight, that he was a natural tennis player. When they finished the beginning lessons, he signed up for the intermediate, then the advanced course. He became so captivated with tennis that he formed an indoor tennis league with some of his co-workers. This move proved to have a hidden byproduct. Through netliving with the tennis participants, on-the-job aspects of his human resources position became amplified, positively modified and simplified as a direct result of the routine relationships formed simply on the tennis courts.

About the time Richard began playing tennis, he also took up jogging. At first it was just for exercise, but one of his friends from the computer department and tennis group was a competitive runner. Jim, an amateur athlete invited Richard to compete in a ten kilometer race. He helped Richard train so that he would not get injured during his first competition. For months they ran about thirty miles a week. They ran a few preliminary races in preparation for the "big one."

The day of the anticipated race finally arrived, and Richard and his computer buddy arrived a half hour early at the race site. They completed their warm-up stretches and limbering exercises just as the race was to begin. Jim got off to a jack rabbit start and disappeared in the crowd, but Richard lagged, pacing himself for the six plus miles.

Richard was hanging in there doing better than he expected until the last 5,000 yards of the race. A hill with a grade of thirty degrees formed the last grueling stretch. Richard despaired; he would have to give up. Meanwhile, his computer friend, far out ahead by then doubled back on the race course and paced himself alongside Richard's faltering steps. His words of encouragement, possibly admonishment, brought to the fore Richard's hidden reserves of stamina and the all-important will to finish. He kept telling himself. "Just one step at a time, keep picking them up and putting them down." This was the mantra that took him through the finish line.

The overall feeling of accomplishment when they crossed that finish line was one of great joy and satisfaction for Richard. He had met the challenge and finished the race. And, he had encountered a true friend, one that put a friend's needs ahead of his own ego drive. In that fact alone lies one of the greatest netliving lessons: "You never stand so tall as when you stoop to help a friend."

Following the race, Richard went directly home and took a nap. He had no idea what his race time was or in what order he had finished. The next morning Jim greeted him in the coffee shop at work eagerly holding out the morning newspaper that proclaimed Richard had won the silver medal for his age group. Richard was elated, but it was some time before he recovered from the shock.

Jim and Richard continued to play tennis and jogged together but no more ten-k races for Richard. Jim was also interested in real estate investments and Richard had done some profitable real estate investing so they spent many hours together talking strategy.

In the fall of that year, Richard joined an executive MBA program put on by a local university so that he could update his skills and broaden his understanding of the business world. His real hope was that he could teach on a college level as an adjunct professor with the advanced degree.

As Richard finished the critical work on his MBA, he began thinking intensely of the retirement stage of his life. Since he was approaching his fifties he felt there was much to consider at this important point. There were such matters as estate planning, legal questions, financial security, and the impact the tax structure would have on his financial retirement plans.

Richard decided that it would be wise for he and Patty to attend some seminars (offered without charge) on these subjects, and so began the netliving process in this new area of interest.

NETLIVING NOTES:

* Netliving will enhance your awareness as you pass through the stages of life. I've learned that I need no formal knowledge just a conscious effort to open myself to whatever comes.
* Netliving will allow you to balance your life between labor, learning and leisure. I've learned that our background and circumstances may have influenced who we are, but we are responsible for who we become.
* Netliving will improve your ability to select role models. I've learned that heroes are the people who do what has to be

done when it needs to be done, regardless of the consequences.

CHAPTER THREE

TO THE ART OF PUBLIC SPEAKING

"Take a chance! All life is a chance. The man who goes furthest is generally the one who is willing to do and dare."

Dale Carnegie (1888-1955)

On a scale of one to ten, fear of public speaking generally ranks at least a nine. In Roberta's case it ranked up there with anticipation of one's death or that of a spouse. She had always been a shy child and as she matured she was considered "reserved." This feeling of wanting to melt into the walls and not be the center of attention was constantly with her.

During high school and college, this continued to be a problem when she had to make presentations in front of the class. Sleepless nights preceded such presentations. She had trouble controlling her eating when public speaking opportunities were a necessary part of the agenda.

In college she took the required course in public speaking and received a passing grade, but she was far from comfortable giving a speech in front of a crowd of strangers. When hired by IBM in their management training program, her manager soon discovered that she did not like to be the center of attention.

As her luck would have it, Roberta's supervisor was a part-time Dale Carnegie speech instructor. He encouraged her to attend an open-house Dale Carnegie session and observe the process first hand. After much coaxing and cajoling she reluctantly went with him, "just to observe."

Much to her surprise, Roberta felt at ease with the group and signed up that night for the fourteen-week course. At the first session she was given three books to use in the course: the RED BOOK, which outlined the assignments, Dale Carnegie's famous HOW TO WIN FRIENDS AND INFLUENCE PEOPLE, PUBLIC SPEAKING INFLUENCING MEN IN BUSINESS, and HOW TO STOP WORRYING AND START LIVING. It was explained that there were inexpensive prizes to be awarded each week. An award was given for the best speech and one for the person showing the most improvement from the previous week. The instructor tactfully explained that there was to be no profanity or vulgarity in these sessions.

At the first session six students were called to the front of the class and asked to sit on a table to make them feel more comfortable. They were seated shoulder to shoulder facing the audience. While they were seated on the table the students were asked to give their first talk by telling about themselves. They were instructed to give their name and address, where they worked, and what kind of work they were doing. They were to indicate how they heard about the course, what they were expecting to obtain from the course, and if they had ever spoken in public before. All the students wore name tags to facilitate the "getting acquainted" process. One of Dale Carnegie's gems is, "A person's name is the most beautiful sound in the world to them, so make sure you say it and spell it correctly."

Roberta found the early sessions concentrated on overcoming fear, and the subject matter of the talks more general than later in the course. One of these early talks called for relating an incident from childhood.

At the third session, students were asked to bring an exhibit to class and explain its use, a grown up "show and tell." Roberta brought her favorite tennis racket. She enjoyed demonstrating the serve and the forehand and backhand strokes. She was happy when she received a large round of applause.

Her next assignment was to speak about an incident from her past that taught her a lesson. Roberta related the story of being lost in a large city and being helped by a kind person. From the start she was encouraged to begin the process of self-examination and to speak on subjects she had earned the right to speak about.

The fifth session was Roberta's favorite and she still remembers it vividly. The class is warmed up with special drills and then the room is prepared for action. A table is set up in front and the speaker is given a tightly rolled newspaper and told to hammer it on the table while talking about some issue that sends the blood pressure off the chart. At the same time the other class members heckle the speaker, who attempts to drown them out with pounding and shouting. This was the best she had ever felt in front of a crowd.

It was during the final session that Roberta listened to one of the most touching stories she had ever heard. The talk was delivered by a middle-aged Japanese-American who was forced to live in an internment camp in Utah during the Second World War because of his Japanese lineage. The feelings and emotions he expressed as he told how he, his mother, father and younger brother were treated by the authorities made the audience squirm. He told how he later fought for his country in the Korean War and how, eventually he became a noted architect. Coincidentally, he had designed an addition to the library on the campus of Roberta's alma mater.

Roberta tried hard to put into everyday practice the principles she had learned from the Dale Carnegie course. It was difficult at first but as time passed it became easier and easier to practice the procedures learned in the lessons. She had even given some thought to becoming a Dale Carnegie instructor but constraints on her time would not permit it.

Instead, through netliving with some of her fellow workers, she got them talking about putting a Toastmasters Club together. This would help her improve her newly learned skills and at the same time help do some netliving within her corporation.

Roberta mentioned her idea of forming a Toastmasters Club to her brother, Richard while sitting around the dinning room table after a great roast beef dinner. One of his pals in the neighborhood belonged to such a club so he volunteered to pick his brains and get back to her.

In laying out her plan, Roberta did research through netliving with some of the old timers in the firm. She learned that about five years before a group had formed a Toastmasters Club but it lasted only a year. Now she was more determined that ever to have a new, successful club.

Before she took any bold steps that might "rock the boat," Roberta confided her plans to her supervisor. Being a strong supporter of public speaking, he was impressed and suggested she talk with the Vice President of Human Resources. The meeting with the VP revealed that he had been involved with the original Toastmasters Club and regretted that it had gone "by the board." He was supportive and offered to grant a half-hour of company time per week for the meetings, provided the participating employees gave up a half-hour of their private time. He also gave Roberta some insight into the factors involved with the failure of the original club --the meeting time was critical, for one. The original club had met right after work on Wednesdays. This created a dilemma for the mothers in the group who had latch-key kids at home waiting for them. Also, he pointed out that the company failed to support the club by not contributing any time for the project.

Through netliving, Roberta found another "old timer" who had been in the original club and was enthusiastic enough about Toastmasters that she had joined an outside club after the original company sponsored club was disbanded. She was a ball of fire and excited with the possibility that a new company club was being considered. She helped Roberta form a charter group of club members to help solicit other potential members for the new club. The Toastmaster organization stipulates that there be a least twenty members before an official Toastmaster Club may be chartered.

Applying netliving, Roberta contacted the local Toastmasters organization and learned of another company club nearby. She phoned the club's president and asked if he would mind helping get the club off the ground. He was delighted to come and help set the club in motion.

In the meantime her brother, Richard had gotten back to her with a glowing report from his neighbor about the benefits of belonging to Toastmasters. This gave further encouragement to Roberta and she could tell by his voice that Richard was also hooked.

At the first steering committee meeting, Roberta suggested that the meeting time for the club be at noon on Wednesdays. This time would satisfy everyone's requirements -- mothers with children at home, as well as those with early work schedules.

Noon until 12:30 p.m. covered regular lunch period paid for by the company, and the 12:30 p.m. until 1:00 p.m. period comprised the half-hour of training time allowed by the V.P. of Human Resources.

An additional selling point the company afforded to members was to consider the semiannual dues covered under the company's tuition refund program. Therefore, the individual members of the Toastmaster club paid only twenty-five percent of the cost to participate in a program that was to pay lifelong dividends for them.

Armed with these new rules and amenities the charter committee was able to attract twenty-five new members, five more that the twenty stipulated by the V.P. of Human Resources and by Toastmasters. Roberta and her core group of fledgling Toastmasters continued to nurture the new venture through netliving.

One of the initial jokes Roberta heard about Toastmasters stated that once you had joined the organization you would become competent in toasting all types of bread . . . such as white, rye, whole wheat, etc. The real reason for the name Toastmaster is that members learn to make succinct toasts at weddings and other public occasions, orally honoring key person or persons.

All the appropriate forms and papers were finally filed and "Food for Thought" Toastmasters Club was officially chartered. At the first meeting the club elected officers and Roberta was elected Public Relations Vice President. Her responsibilities included promoting the best features of the club to the work force and conducting the ongoing membership drive.

At the first meeting the club also decided: THE MISSION OF THE "FOOD FOR THOUGHT" CLUB shall read as follows: "The mission of a Toastmasters club is to provide a mutually supportive and positive learning environment in which every member has the opportunity to develop communication and leadership skills, which in turn foster self-confidence and personal growth."

The club officers reviewed the different tasks that each member of the club volunteers to perform at the weekly meetings. First on the agenda is the INVOCATOR, who stands up after being introduced by the TOASTMASTER and recites a prayer, a quotation, a saying or short story. Afterwards he or she leads the Pledge of Allegiance by facing the United States flag and holding the right hand above the heart.

The duties of the TOASTMASTER:

Prior to the meeting: Contact the invocator, Speakers and the General Evaluator to find out if they will be attending or if they have a substitute. Advise the secretary of any changes by 11:00 a.m. on the day of the meeting. Prepare introductions for each Speaker and the General Evaluator and announce speech titles, speech numbers, purpose, and time allowed. Information about each member can be obtained from the Bio book maintained by the President. The TOASTMASTER sets the tone of the meeting and acts as host, leading greetings and applause when introducing a member or when a speech or responsibility is completed.

At the meeting: When introduced, he or she approaches the lectern and shakes hands with the President. When introducing the speakers, prepare the audience for what is to come. Always shake hands with the speaker as he/she approaches the lectern.

The duties of the TOPICMASTER: Greet the Toastmaster and the audience. State the theme or topic. Remind everyone about the "word of the day." Pick members not doing a specific job to briefly participate in the topics. Turn the meeting back over to the Toastmaster. Wait at the lectern and shake the Toastmaster's hand before sitting down.

The duties of the GENERAL EVALUATOR: Prior to the meeting: Contact the Evaluators, Grammarian, Ah Counter and Timer. Confirm attendance -- make substitutions as necessary. Call secretary the morning of the meeting to confirm the agenda.

At the Meeting: Greet the Toastmaster, members and any guests. Introduce the Evaluator for each Speaker -- names only. Add pertinent observations not addressed by the Evaluator. Ask for reports from the Timer, The Ah Counter and the Grammarian. Evaluate the general conduct of the entire meeting. Return the meeting to the Toastmaster.

The duties of the EVALUATOR: Prior to the meeting: Contact the assigned speakers to determine the title, speech number and specific areas to look for during the speech. Consult the manual for speech that you are evaluating. At the meeting: As you begin your report: Greet the General Evaluator and address the audience. Give pertinent oral and written evaluations. Always offer ideas for improvement and positive feedback.

The role of the TIMER: When called upon to report: Greet the General Evaluator and address the audience. Be prepared to time the Speakers, Table topic participants and the Evaluation. Make certain the timing device is in clear view of each speaker and participant. Report each participant's name and time used.

The duties of the AH COUNTER: When called upon to report: Greet the General Evaluator and address the audience. Throughout the meeting, listen for sounds and long pauses used as fillers. Mention if the person's use of fillers is over or under five. After the meeting, meet with individuals who wish to discuss delivery.

The role of the GRAMMARIAN: Prior to the meeting: Post the "Word of the Day." For each person who takes the floor make note of usage of the "Word of the Day", proper or colorful word usage, and/or repeated lapses of grammar. When called upon by the General Evaluator, greet the General Evaluator and address the audience. Give a brief report based on your observations. Turn the meeting over to the General Evaluator. After the meeting, review specific notes with individuals as appropriate.

Roberta threw herself into mastering this dynamic endeavor with total enthusiasm. What she especially liked about Toastmasters was that they had a plan and step-by-step directions to achieve success. The first goal of a new Toastmaster member is to become a CTM (Competent ToastMaster). This goal may be accomplished by giving a series of ten speeches.

Each of the ten speeches has a specific purpose. The first speech, "The Ice Breaker" begins your speaking experience by talking about the subject closest to you -- yourself. In the process of introducing yourself to your fellow club members, you provide insight into your background, interests and ambitions.

As you prepare and deliver your talk, you will become aware of communication skills you already possess and areas that require some improvement. Your fellow members will help you understand these needs, as they see them. Thus the netliving aspects of this program are strong and provide the essence of its success.

Roberta prepared for her initial speech by looking first at the objectives. The objectives were: To begin speaking before an audience, to understand what areas require particular emphasis in developing speaking skills, and to make a self-introduction to her fellow club members.

Roberta had only four to six minutes to present her personal profile. She selected three or four interesting aspects of her life that would give insight and provide understanding of her as an individual. She would include her birthplace, that she is a twin, the facts about her family and information about her formal education. She would also share how she came to be in her present occupation, and further mention her future ambitions.

As Roberta had learned in her Dale Carnegie course, a good speech needs an opening, a body and a conclusion. She wanted to create an interesting opening sentence to hook the attention of the audience immediately. Next she thought of the conclusion. Having a good start and a solid finish, she could easily fill in the body of the speech.

Roberta knew that a "smart talk" contains only a few main points. These would be expanded through examples, stories and anecdotes. She knew from prior experience that people will not remember a point unless it is repeated and restated, but they will easily recall a story long after the speech is completed.

Roberta prepared herself by reviewing her notes and practicing until she felt comfortable. She did not have to memorize her speech, she already knew the subject well. However, she did memorize the opening and closing sentences. The opener and closer she felt were vital keys.

Next, she persuaded her brother to act as a dry run audience and give her feedback on presentation and content. She also recorded the talk and listened to it carefully, making improvements she felt were necessary. Roberta found using a tape recorder one of the best ways to improve public speaking ability. Playing the recording over and over while reading the speech outline involved two of her five senses and helped her remember the sequence and the inflections.

Roberta found it helpful to think of this presentation as talking to a group of friends, sharing information of interest, rather than the rigorous "making a speech." A great feature of netliving toward better speaking with fellow toastmasters was sharing the common experience. The anticipation, the fear, the nervousness, the desire to succeed and the eagerness to help was common throughout the group.

Always well groomed and appropriately dressed for work, Roberta was properly attired for the presentation. She learned some time ago that when you look right, you feel good about yourself. She could forget her appearance and concentrate on presenting her talk. Her Father always reminded her on such occasions, "Roberta, you never get a second chance to make a good first impression on people."

In talking to some of the seasoned Toastmasters, Roberta heard that feeling a bit nervous is common to every speaker, no matter how experienced. Some nervousness at the beginning of a speech promotes enthusiasm and excitement. Taking a few deep breaths and slowly exhaling while being introduced is always a good idea and will assist the voice in sounding resonant and natural. The old timers also suggested that while speaking, she make "eye contact" with members of the audience. By looking directly at one person for a few seconds and moving on to another, the audience feels a connection to the speaker. Roberta was instructed to keep her hands at her side and not wave them all over the place. Later she would learn how to use "body language" to stress points and convey different messages to her audience. She was also told not to conclude the talk by saying, "thank you." as many people are inclined to do. The audience should be thanking the speaker for the information just shared.

When Roberta finished the presentation and sat in her chair, she began to evaluate her performance. She could have smiled more, she had missed some vital points, she had said a few "ahs." Then one of the experienced members stood up and evaluated her talk. She was complimentary of Roberta's overall performance and felt she had done a great job for an "Ice Breaker." She went on to compliment Roberta on her diction and use of words. Then came the curve ball -- she had used an excessive amount of "ahs." The actual count was thirty one.

In the years that followed, Roberta's speech making talent grew. After completing the ten required speeches for her CTM, she mastered the advanced manuals and became more and more involved with the Toastmaster program. Her success with the program inspired her brother, Richard to join his neighborhood Toastmasters Club.

There was only one dark cloud that appeared in the sky while the new "Food for Thought" Toastmasters club was being chartered. One of the secretaries who had been a member of the original toastmaster club that failed went out of her way to attempt to sabotage the newly formed club. Little things like scheduling meetings in the conference room at noon on Wednesdays when she knew that was the normal meeting time for the new club.

Through patience and flexibility the new club worked around these inconveniences and finally she gave up and moved on to another employer.

NETLIVING NOTES:

* Netliving will increase your risk taking. I've learned that you shouldn't compare yourself to the best others can do, but to the best you can do.
* Netliving will improve your ability to win friends and influence people. I've learned that true friendship continues to grow, even over the longest distance.

* Netliving will enhance your public speaking and self-image. I've learned that it's taking me a long time to become the person I want to be.

CHAPTER FOUR

FOR A MENTOR

"If we have the mistaken idea that, in order to be an adult and mature, we need to go it alone, we should remember that even the most successful and talented athletes have coaches who guide, encourage, and instruct them. We need coaches too. It is important we learn from the example of others who have successfully been down the road we are traveling."

Sue Patton Thoele

One warm fall afternoon, Richard hurried across the university campus on his way to an interview for yet another part-time job. Recently discharged from the U.S. Navy after serving four years as a high speed radio operator, he struggled to survive. Uncle Sam's educational stipend, paid to Korean Conflict GI's who opted to attend college, was stretched thin. Supplemental income became vital. Hence this "future astronaut" humbled himself to accept menial jobs to realize his dream of one day going up in space.

The year was 1957. The Russians had launched "Sputnik" and caught the world's attention. Richard was among many young Americans determined not to allow Russia to dominate space. His waking hours were spent studying physics and dreaming of riding a rocket to the moon,. The former first class naval petty officer made the difficult transition to a lowly, beanie wearing college freshman in search of part-time work.

The ad stated that a "driver" was needed. Richard had driven everything from a motor scooter to a navy bus, but the job turned out to require more than "driving." The boss was a forty-eight year old real estate tycoon, paralyzed from the neck down as a result of polio contracted when he was a nineteen-year-old university student. At six feet two and two hundred pounds, he was an imposing individual even though wheelchair bound. He had been an ace tennis player in top physical condition when the disease struck. His physical strength and strong spirituality probably saved his life.

As the employment interview progressed, Richard's comfort level gradually increased. He discovered they shared an Irish-American heritage and a deep faith in God. The two men talked at length. It was agreed that Richard had the maturity necessary to assist with the daily personal hygiene requirements in addition to the advertised driving tasks.

Over the course of Richard's college years the two men formed a deep bond. Richard admired his boss's brilliant mind. He was talented and resourceful. His ability to remember names and phone numbers was impressive. Using only the index finger on his right hand he dialed the numbers stored in his well-trained memory. He freely discussed philosophical and theological ideas with Richard and thus became a powerful mentor.

Encouraged by such a positive influence, Richard developed mentally and expanded his business concepts while achieving his immediate supplemental financial goals.

The summer between Richard's freshman and sophomore year he met his future in-laws. His future wife's parents, Tim and Betty Murphy, had met his boss at a church function and they had become friends. They were visiting at his home one evening when they met Richard and took an immediate liking to him. There were many similarities in family backgrounds. In fact, there was a common ancestry line back to Ireland.

Tim Murphy had just been transferred to New York City and the family was in the process of relocating to that area of the country. The Murphy's elder daughter, Patricia, had spent the summer working for her uncle at an oceanfront resort hotel. At the end of the summer she would return home and attend college. In the fall she was greeted by the news that she had to pass her driver's examination so she could help with family chores. She was also informed that her parents had secured the services of an "old" navy vet to teach her how to drive.

His new student and Richard met and disliked one another instantly. However, she was under direct orders from her parents, and he needed the money. So, they made the most of a seemingly difficult situation. Tim Murphy owned a Buick Century that had seen better days, but there was no way Richard was going to use his personal car to teach this coed how to drive.

On the first driving lesson he attempted to explain to his student the fundamentals of driving and the use of the various controls behind the wheel. Richard made it clear to her that when he told her to hit the breaks she needed to listen closely and respond with enthusiasm since the Buick was not equipped with dual controls commonly found on training vehicles.

Mrs. Murphy had much compassion for this young man who was working so hard to become successful. She felt sorry for him that he had to eat his dinner at those hamburger restaurants so she began inviting him to have supper with the family. Since Mr. Murphy was in New York City on his new job there was an extra chair at the table. This was a huge treat for a poor college boy who missed his mother's home cooking.

Patricia had three younger brothers and a younger sister. The boys especially enjoyed teasing the "big guy." Tim Junior, her oldest brother was the most creative tease. He would place a "whoopee cushion" on Richard's chair just as he was sitting down and the ensuing noise caused some embarrassment to the guest.

Another favorite trick was for Tim Junior to crawl under the table and tie Richard's shoelaces together. Hence when he would attempt to leave the table at the end of the meal he would trip and that would create great laughter among the children.

Gradually the student and teacher relationship improved and they began dating. They continued the "driver's training program" and Richard used to tease Patricia that she was ready to take the driver's exam but she still insisted that her parking was not up to par. She eventually took the driver's test and passed it with flying colors. They went to all the formal dances together that year and in the beginning of their junior year became engaged. The romance had been a stormy one from the beginning. Richard was five years older than she but at times he acted much more immature. He would fly into an angry burst with the slightest provocation. It seemed that becoming engaged seemed to throw more gasoline on the fire for he became more difficult for Patricia to understand.

Finally, just before the Christmas holiday after an evening of tremendous stress and arguing she gave him his engagement ring back and they went their separate ways. They did not see or hear from each other for several years.

While all this chaos was going on, Richard's chores and academic responsibilities continued as did Patricia's. When mastering math proved difficult, Richard aligned himself with a young freshman. This physics and math whiz was nicknamed "Rockets." He too had a dream of landing on the moon. The peace-loving whiz and the trained vet became tutor and bodyguard.

After a full year of employment as a driver and caregiver, Richard followed his boss' advice to study for his real estate license. Thus began years of part-time real estate sales combined with the original responsibilities of employment. Richard learned to search out prospects for real estate listings. Driving different routes home from the office each night, the two men surveyed various neighborhoods for real estate opportunities as they passed through. Richard's powers of observation were sharply honed under the watchful eye of the real estate pro. Richard matched his abilities against the trained mind of his highly experienced mentor. He learned to spot opportunities and remember details, to plan strategy and to negotiate real estate matters. But most of all, Richard learned to appreciate the dignity of work.

During this period a distinct personal relationship also grew. Richard was there when his boss met and fell in love with his future wife. As "driver," he was a key player in the romance between the paraplegic and the young businesswoman. The courtship opened up new conversations between the two men. They discussed morality and relationships. They shared insights and advice. Richard was impressed by his boss' respect for women. He heard the echo of his father's words, "Richard, treat other girls the way you would want a guy to treat your sister." This really struck a note with him when he first heard it because he was crazy about his sister, Roberta and could not conceive of a man mistreating her.

One of the difficulties the courtship presented for Richard was waiting outside in the cold weather, night after night, while his mentor and the girlfriend were discussing wedding plans. This lasted for almost a full year.

Following the wedding, Richard continued to serve as driver while pursuing his real estate career. He found the work exciting and enjoyed dealing with an ever widening group of people. His fellow salespeople and his clients further broadened his netliving insight.

A year after the big wedding there were signs that a "miracle child" was going to enter their lives. The doctors and medical experts had predicted there was only a slim chance that Richard's boss could father a child, but he proved them wrong. At the age of thirty-nine, his wife gave birth to a bouncing baby girl. He was fifty-one at the time.

The time period leading to the birth was a joyous one for Richard. He and the other driver made dry runs to the hospital to practice what they would do when the "time" arrived. Richard's boss was a nervous wreck and had the other members of his team on "red alert" most of the time.

As fate so often decrees, Richard was back home in Pennsylvania for the Thanksgiving holiday when the little bundle decided to make her appearance. The other driver and Richard flipped a coin to determine who would drive and who would hold the baby on the way home from the hospital. The other driver won the toss. While Richard drove, a burly football player filled the back seat, holding a tiny pink bundle of joy.

During the ensuing months, Richard spent many mornings feeding and rocking the baby. Since Richard had only his twin sister, no younger brothers or sisters, this baby was a unique experience. He discovered how much he really liked little babies. This strong affection for babies continued throughout the rest of his life.

When Richard had the opportunity he would call his sister Roberta and tell her all about the new baby and what was going on in his life and catch up on how his sister was getting along.

Time progressed and it became apparent to Richard that he was not going to be taking that rocket ride to the moon. He had shown a strong interest in the business world and advanced calculus helped him decide that he was not cut out to be a scientist. He decided to pursue a career in the corporate world and left the real estate business behind. The real estate license expired, but the netliving and mentoring lessons never died.

In fact, as Richard progressed in his corporate career in the human resource area, he became quite involved in the mentoring concept. He learned that the origin of mentoring was found in Greek Mythology. Mentor was the Greek educator who taught Homer's children. The current definition of mentoring: "One developmental, caring, sharing and helpful relationship where one person invests time, know-how, and effort in enhancing another person's growth, knowledge, skills, and responds to critical needs in the life of that person in ways that prepares the individual for greater productivity or achievement in the future."

Richard became a student of mentoring and found there were three basic types of mentoring or ways to mentor. First there were the situational "short bursts," where mentor and student are brought together for short, isolated episodes. This type of mentoring is spontaneous, off the cuff. It appears to be random and often casual, creative or innovative. For example, one of Richard's neighbors, who had been a professional golf caddie all his life, took him to the local driving range. In the hour it took to hit a large bucket of balls, his neighbor had taught him three little changes to make in his swing that eventually removed eight strokes from Richard's game.

The second type is the "informal" and is the "most common" form of mentoring. It is strictly voluntary and personal. The mentor is quite responsive to the student's needs. It is loosely structured and flexible mentoring.

"Formal" or "Organizational Sponsored" is the third type of mentoring. The hallmark of this type is that it is goal-oriented. It is driven by organizational needs. Richard found there is a formal arrangement for matching mentor and student. What usually starts as a formal, controlled system turns into a strong friendship and leads to an ongoing, long-term, positive netliving relationship.

Since Richard had been placed in charge of the mentorship program at his company, he felt it would be a good idea for him to become a mentor to know and experience first-hand what the program was all about. His firm's program was a bit different than other for-profit organizations inasmuch as the mentoring was not taking place within the corporate structure but at an adopted inner-city middle school.

The program was designed to help students who, in most cases, were coming from one parent homes to have a person they could count on to give them advice, listen to their problems, and hopefully direct them to the right career.

Richard found there are several stages to mentoring: Attraction, personal disclosure, bonding, distance, revisiting the relationship, peer mentoring, reciprocity, and closure. There are also roles for the mentor and the student.

The mentor's role is first to ask, What are the most important things I would like to get from this relationship? Then the mentor must indicate the areas he/she is best at and determine whether they are of particular interest to the student. What is the student's preferred method of learning? (Shadowing, listening, hands-on.) How can I, as a mentor, increase the comfort area between us? What do I need to know about you right now? What is important to you?

The student's role is to indicate the areas that need to be strengthened. I have set the following personal development plans I want to achieve -- is this on target or reachable? List of the subjects I need to know more about. Here are some things you should know about me.

Then Richard brought up the question of logistics: How often will we meet? How long will our meetings last? Where will we meet? Who is responsible for setting our meetings? How do we go about canceling a scheduled meeting? What is the best method of contacting each other?

His student wanted to know what ideas he had about getting organized. What if we want to change our agreement (contract)? Both pointed out that a pitfall of mentoring can occur when the expectations of the mentor and the student are unrealistic. The other area of concern to both is a breach of confidentiality.

The benefits from participating in this mentorship program for Richard were many. He found it validated many of his own ideas. He received much personal gratification and growth from the experience. There was a sense of being needed that Richard had not experienced before. It gave him an opportunity for self-examination while teaching his student.

Richard's student expressed appreciation for the guidance he had received in addition to the opportunity to learn new skills. There was also a decrease in stress once the socialization process was underway. He also expressed a stronger sense of direction which gave him a stronger feeling of security.

This experience reminded Richard of the many mentors he himself had along his life's journey, and netliving with them had helped him improve in all aspects of his life. During this time period Richard had experienced a serious family tragedy. His closest first cousin had been killed in an auto/truck accident on the Pennsylvania Turnpike. He was so upset that he reached for the phone and called Patricia in New York and she flew out on the next plane.

Within six months they had a big church wedding and had three healthy and happy children over the next six years.

NETLIVING NOTES:

* Netliving will enhance your ability to mentor. I've learned that it's not what you have, but what you give away that counts.
* Netliving will improve your business skills. I've learned that two heads are better than one in any business situation.
* Netliving will help your spiritual development. I've learned that when there are two or more gathered in God's Name there is spiritual growth.

CHAPTER FIVE

FOR FINANCIAL SUCCESS

"It is no longer our resources that limit our decisions; it's our decisions that limit our resources."

U. Thant (1909-1974)

It all began in a financial class in an executive MBA program in the late seventies. When the finance professor introduced the subject of "dollar averaging," Roberta chimed in, voicing her experience in forming an investment club after undergraduate training.

Don, the fellow who sat next to her in class, was interested in the stock market as an abstract idea, but had never seriously studied it or invested in any stock. After class, he approached Roberta and began questioning her about the stock market in general, and the possibility of forming an investment club.

Roberta and this inquisitive fellow student stopped at the campus coffee shop for a break, where she related her investment club story.

Several members of the corporate staff of the truck manufacturing company where Roberta was employed liked the idea of an investment club and were eager to give it a shot. The general accountant in her office had a friend, who worked for one of the then "big eight" accounting firms, who was also interested in the idea. Roberta, a sociology major working in human resources, was leading a general accountant, a senior staff accountant, a tax accountant, and an auditor into their financial future. It was a classic example of a "broad brush" person leading a group of narrowly focused individuals.

Roberta's apartment was the scene of the initial organization meeting, and she kept the coffee coming as they explored the merits of traveling down the road of investing. Besides the accounting types present at the meeting, there was also a friend of hers from the insurance industry and her brother Richard. They talked at great length regarding goals and whether or not to become a legal partnership. The group decided it would be a good idea to invite one of the young attorneys from the corporate staff to the next meeting. He would be able to give them a slant on the legal intricacies of forming an investment club.

Most of the members were people with backgrounds similar to Roberta's, struggling junior executives without a lot of spendable income for investment speculation. They decided to start small -- twenty-five dollar monthly contribution by each member.

The subject of joining the National Association of Investment Clubs was raised by one of the members who had read about it in Reader's Digest. That member volunteered to research the subject at the public library and report back to the club at the next meeting. It was also decided to keep minutes of each meeting on a rotating basis so that no one member would be overburdened with all the record-keeping. In order to make it convenient for most of the club members, it was decided to hold future meetings in one of the corporate conference rooms.

These monthly meetings continued for approximately five years. They all took place in the same conference room of the company's headquarters. The second meeting of the East Side Investment Club, as it was now known, was attended by the young attorney who explained the difference between forming a legal partnership and a Sub Chapter S corporation. The members discussed the pros and cons at length and decided to form a partnership under the state's laws. The young attorney indicated he would draw up all the legal paperwork for two hundred dollars. For the members of the club this amount seemed exorbitant. They debated back and forth the balance of the meeting and finally voted to proceed.

Roberta's friend from the insurance company, who had the most knowledge and experience of investing, decided she could not afford to participate. The same decision was reached by her brother. Another member was so excited about the concept he wanted to double the monthly amount of investment. He was able to convince the group that they needed a certain amount of cash in order to buy round lots (one hundred shares) versus odd lots (less than one hundred.) There was a significant monetary advantage to buying round lots instead of odd lots. A vote was taken and to everyone's amazement, it passed unanimously. The club was off to a skyrocket start moving from an investment amount of twenty-five collars to fifty dollars a month at only its second meeting.

The report on the National Association of Investment Clubs was presented and the members decided to join. This organization would provide powerful tools to use in making decisions regarding which stocks to purchase.

It was like Christmas when the first package of materials arrived from the NAIC headquarters in Detroit, Michigan. There were stock study guides and P/E ratio charts. Also enclosed was a copy of Better Investing, with the stock of the month on the cover. Better Investing was the monthly magazine of the NAIC.

Each member chose a stock to study for the next monthly meeting. One member was to make a detailed presentation and recommend a stock for the club's prospective investment.

The tax professional member volunteered to keep the partnership's books. His duties were to log all receipts and write checks from the partnership account in payment of stocks purchased. He also prepared and filed year-end tax forms. He managed to keep the club in the black the entire time it was in existence.

With the passage of time, the auditor from the "big eight" firm, Pete, mastered the tools of NAIC. He purchased many investment oriented books and became a self-taught expert with the tools of financial analysis. Pete began attending local meetings of NAIC and then graduated to regional meetings and eventually went to the national convention as a guest speaker. He was a great asset to the investment club. Pete studied not only the stock he was assigned but many others. His personal investments met with such success he was able to afford long desired flying lessons and eventually his own aircraft. He then flew all over the country giving lectures on how to invest in the stock market using material from the National Association of Investment Clubs.

Although Roberta's East Side Investment Club prospered from the knowledge gained by Pete's efforts and the club profited from the stocks he recommended, the ugly green eye of jealousy appeared. Some of the other members of the club resented his success. They felt he had more than one vote when it came to selecting stocks. Ironically the member who introduced him to the club was the most critical of him.

Roberta had to have one-on-one private discussions with these disgruntled members and remind them of the success the club had experienced from Pete's efforts. The return on investment was an amazing thirty to forty percent. The chosen stocks were all winners. She reminded them that the goal of the investment club was to make money for each member and we did not have to love each member, but we did need to respect each person for his/her efforts.

After looking at the facts and allowing the emotions to subside the members decided to raise the monthly club dues to a hundred dollars-- the club was on a roll. The members felt so successful that they wanted to move beyond stock investing and get into the real estate market to make some "real" money.

The club decided to target vacant land that could be purchased relatively cheap, held and then sold later to a developer or eventually even to be developed by the club. This was a plausible concept, though a bit more risky since real estate did not move as quickly as the stock market. Roberta was the only one in the club who had experience in buying real estate. She had worked her way through college selling real estate part-time for a local broker. She volunteered to research some parcels of land and report to the club at the next meeting. Roberta decided to look at farm country where the land prices were relatively cheap.

Roberta decided one plot of land she looked at had potential. It was located on the corner of a state limited access highway and a major two-lane road. The prime watchword of the real estate industry, "LOCATION, LOCATION, LOCATION," fully applied to her selection; forty acres, planted in pine trees.

Roberta enthusiastically reported her findings at the next monthly meeting and urged the group to make a first-hand inspection of the property. None of the other members would look at it. They were too preoccupied with personal business and strongly felt that the club should buy it sight unseen, based on Roberta's recommendation.

After days of discussion and deliberation, Roberta decided not to make the offer. Some of the reasons for this decision had to do with the pressure it would have put on her shoulders. Even though the other members had given her the authority, if things did not go well there was bound to be a lot of second guessing. At the next monthly meeting she explained her feelings about the predicament to the group and they understood. That was the end of the club's fling at the real estate market. Roberta confessed later that if she had possessed the ability to raise enough money, she would have purchased the plot of land herself.

The plot of land recommended for the club turned out to be loaded with oil and gas. Years later, while Roberta was driving to visit a friend at a nearby lake, she observed the oil rigs pumping away. SUCH IS LIFE, she thought.

As the years passed, the club members grew to know each other well and learned to trust each other explicitly. After conquering the initial jealousy, all the members were fond of Pete, the "flying" representative of NAIC. He had contributed a great deal toward the success of the club. One cold wintry evening, Roberta received a phone call from his father telling her there had been an accident and Pete, the pilot, was dead.

He had been flying into Oil City, Pennsylvania for a speaking engagement for the local chapter of NAIC when his Piper Cub hit high voltage wires. The entire membership of the club attended the wake and funeral service. He had made many friends during his short lifetime. He was a giving person who had built a wide network of close friends. Many of his investment strategy students visited the funeral home to pay their last respects.

Pete's death set off a chain reaction of events, and like a row of dominoes, the members began to drop out of the club. One of the accountants was transferred to Michigan. The club tax person was sent off to sunny California as a full blown tax manager.

When the club dwindled down to two (Roberta and one accountant), they decided to give up on the whole idea. The thought of bringing in new members proved to be too difficult because the shares had appreciated so much over time. New members would have had to come in with an initial investment of twenty-five thousand dollars. After five years of operation, the East Side Investment Club had done exceedingly well and the members walked away with enough money to launch a child's college education. Roberta contacted the attorney and he dissolved the partnership just as he had created it.

Don, Roberta's fellow student in the MBA class became interested in the idea of investing and dogged her for months for information on the National Association of Investment Clubs. She gave him some back copies of Better Investing and he sent away for more data and became obsessed with the stock market. Every time he had a break between classes, he would sit and ask Roberta questions about stocks and bonds.

Don absorbed all the information and a year after graduation he approached Roberta with a new concept on investing. He realized that, as an individual, he could purchase one share of stock in a company which participates in "reinvestment." He then could invest money in that company on a quarterly basis without paying any broker fees. Don carried this concept one step further and traded other individual investors a share of one of his "reinvestment" stocks for one of their "reinvestment" stocks.

The concept was that once the new share was registered in a person's name, that person could buy more shares free of broker's commissions. He became so excited about this concept that he began to write a book and also had articles published in newspapers and magazines. In these articles he explained that over seven hundred companies listed on the New York Stock Exchange participate in "Dividend Reinvestment Programs."

During this time period, Roberta shared this financial knowledge with her brother Richard. He piggy-backed on her experience and turned out to be a fairly sophisticated investor himself.

Since her days in the East Side Investment Club and her discussions with her fellow MBA student, Don. Roberta remained well informed about the changing picture of investing. Now her goal was to concentrate on providing sufficient retirement income.

NETLIVING NOTES:

* Netliving will improve your financial planning ability. I've learned that you can do something in an instant that will give you a heartache for life.
* Netliving will broaden your understanding of investing. I've learned that I must have the willingness to keep an open mind.
* Netliving will help you to reach financial security. I've learned that all things happen in their own time as long as I do the footwork.

FIGURE 6-1

SOURCES OF HUMAN RESOURCES

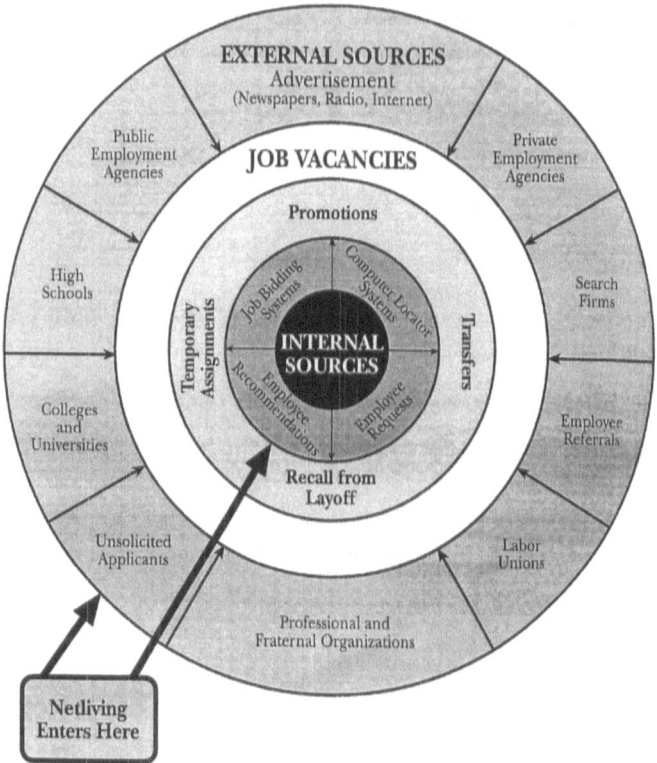

DOUBLE BARRELED APPROACH

Figure 6-1

CHAPTER SIX

CAREER SECRETS

"If we treat people as they are, they will stay as they are. But if we treat them for what they might be, and might become, they will become those better selves."

G.T. Smith (1935-   )

As Richard began his senior year at college, his thoughts focused on his future life and career. He discussed his concerns with his parents and his sister, Roberta. His father suggested meeting with an old family friend who was experienced in the human resource field. A meeting with this professional, who was in charge of the human resource department a local steel mill, was arranged.

Richard left home that Saturday morning with many questions and some symptoms of nervousness. His throat was dry and his hands were moist with perspiration. While growing up, he had met this respected gentleman at company picnics and held him in awe. The meeting was informal. The human resource manager put Richard at ease immediately. He began by asking what kinds of courses he had taken in college. Then he went on to ask about extracurricular activities. The conversation detailed the different types of careers that were flourishing at the time.

The HR professional began talking to Richard about the process of selecting a career. He indicated that when companies are deciding what kind of products they want to make, they look at many areas before they make a final decision. Many consumer products companies look at the demographics to get some clues as to what kinds of products to develop. He told Richard the story of a small family-owned restaurant business. This family had two sons who graduated from a famous business college one year apart. These sons had learned the importance of demographics, so when their father began thinking about going into the frozen dinner business, these boys began looking at the 1950 census report.

They noticed that many women who had gone to work outside the home during World War II never returned to housework. They liked having extra money in their purses and the freedom granted those working in the business world. The two sons interpreted this trend and decided that there would be a strong demand for convenient, easy-to-prepare meals in the near future. Combined with the invention of the microwave oven in the early fifties, the needs of employed homemakers made the frozen dinner business a sure winner.

The rest of the story is well-known. The family began making extra batches of dinners in one of their restaurants and selling them from a freezer chest located in the front lobby. Business mushroomed in a short period of time. In 1954 a vacant neighborhood plant was purchased and production grew in leaps and bounds. Today, they are a billion dollar company.

The HR person emphasized to Richard that there are clues to what the future will bring -- study the present and project where certain decisions, based on clues, will lead. He also pointed out to Richard that he should first think in terms of types of desirable industries. Then narrow the field to two or three selections. Research the strong, well-managed companies within the selected industries. He was quick to indicate that, in his opinion, the steel industry was not growing. With the end of World War II and advent of the Marshall Plan and the rebuilding of Germany and Japan, much of the new technology had been installed in the overseas steel mills and now, by the mid-fifties, the U. S. Steel industry was slowly being overcome by foreign steel.

Another industry indicating early signs of problems was the U.S. auto industry. At one point most Americans would not even consider buying a foreign car. This trend was changing rapidly, and the German Volkswagen "bug" was becoming popular with Americans. In fact, Richard himself owned one. Then, just a few years later, the Japanese auto makers began manufacturing high quality vehicles such as the Honda and Toyota. Their popularity with U.S. car buyers grew steadily.

Thus Richard was advised to discover a vibrant industry that would enjoy many years of growth. Richard asked for examples of such an industry. The HR professional indicated that, in his opinion, the computer industry was one that would see continued growth and would flourish well into the next century. Richard could not argue with that projection. Another recommendation was the food industry. First, people have to eat to live. Secondly, the U. S. has the most powerful food producing system in the world. This production system extends from the greatest per acre agricultural delivery system to the most technically advanced food processing plants. There is also little threat from an "off-shore" competitor.

Richard and the kind gentleman talked for hours about ways to tap into these industries and companies. For the first time Richard heard the term "netliving." The professional explained the process as a method of sharing information in which both parties benefit from the exchange. In his words, it was not a "one-way street." He explained to Richard that you begin by phoning companies and arrange "informational interviews." In such an interview the interviewee refrains from asking the interviewer directly for a job. Asking for the job, in many cases, scares the potential employer and the opportunity for employment may be lost forever.

During the informational interview, Richard had been instructed to find out about the company and its products and to obtain the names of the hiring parties within the organization. In addition, it would be helpful to learn of other companies which were currently hiring. Some people are anxious to tell you what other companies are doing. If a good impression is made at the informational interview, perhaps the hiring party will favorably remember that interview and resume when a "real" interview is appropriate. See Figure 6-1 Sources of Human Resources to determine where netliving enters the picture.

Richard thanked his mentor for all the valuable information and the amount of time he had spent. Back at home he reviewed the day's exciting events with his parents and sister. He told them he planned to become a Human Resource Professional like his father's friend. He would also help young people decide what career path they would follow.

He also went into great detail regarding what he had learned that day about the concept of "netliving" with his sister, Roberta. He explained to her that the concept could be used in all aspects of life not just in the area of finding a job. The main idea of the process was to be proactive and establish the "network" long before it was actually needed. Just like in job searching, it required a planning element as well as an action piece.

Upon arriving on campus that fall, Richard contacted the Placement Office and began doing some netliving with the employees who worked there. However, the Placement Department was of little help to him. One of his professors suggested that he contact the Alumni Office and obtain a copy of the most recent Alumni Directory.

Armed with this resource, Richard began immediately to look in the book for Human Resource Executives to contact. The Directory had code letters for the various occupational categories. He phoned the listed executive and requested an informational interview at an agreed upon time and place. Most executives preferred to conduct these interviews on their site because it saved them time while providing the college student with a view of the real world.

Most of the executives listed in the directory had volunteered to do career netliving with students. They were expecting the calls and were gracious and patient about providing the service. There was a hidden agenda for some of these executives. If they found special candidates among the students, they would receive accolades for bringing in talented new blood. This was an exciting, though scary, time for Richard. With the senior year work load and the time spent on interviewing, he began to wonder how he would ever complete everything on time to graduate and have a job lined up too.

He remembered his father's famous saying: "one step at a time." He proceeded to do just that. He laid out an organized plan every day and was regimented in following through on the tasks that had to be completed for that day.

Richard interviewed with many good companies in a variety of industries. Following the advice of his father's HR friend, he concentrated on the growing industries. He was especially interested in the computer field. He had an on-campus interview with IBM and was impressed with the interviewer. Richard went to the campus library and researched the company thoroughly. He felt they were a strong company in a strong industry and had many great products and programs.

Following the on-campus interview, Richard kept in touch with the individual who had interviewed him. However, using the newly learned netliving approach he uncovered another contact at IBM in the form of a spouse of one of the salespeople in the real estate office that employed him part-time. This source contacted the on-campus interviewer and gave a glowing reference regarding Richard and the hiring process moved along quickly.

Richard's dreams came true when he received the formal letter inviting him to become a management trainee with "The Big Blue." He had several other opportunities, but this was the one that he really wanted to pursue. He decided to join a company with a philosophy that considered each employee an IBMer.

Following graduation he went to work for IBM and became identified as an IBMer with his white shirt, tie and dark suit. The only immediate drawback was that his position did not fall into the planned category of human resources. He had been advised by the IBM recruiter and other company representatives that most college graduates interested in human resources are not hired into that function immediately. Most corporations want the new graduate to get some management experience before moving into human resources responsibilities. This hands-on experience, along with their academic understanding of the field, creates a stronger, more well-rounded and efficient employee.

With this in mind, Richard volunteered for every available activity that was in some way related to the human resource function. When IBM needed someone to lead the savings bond drive, Richard was there. When there was a need for someone to visit a local college campus, Richard's hand was the first to be raised. He was elected to the presidency of the local IBM Club and in this position performed many typical human resource functions and activities.

Richard became more and more eager to be involved in the actual human resource field. As the years passed it became apparent he would need to make some changes if it was to be accomplished within IBM.

That knowledge, combined with the indications that he needed union negotiating experience to be considered a serious human resource professional, meant he would have to leave his beloved union-free IBM.

This decision did not come easy for Richard. He spent many long hours discussing the pros and cons with his sister, Roberta who was currently in grad school. Being in the same field she was a good sounding board since she had been in HR longer because of his four year military obligation. He also discussed it at great lengths with his father who Richard felt had a good feel for work-related topics and great common sense.

Using the netliving skills he learned in college, Richard again set up some "informational interviews." His target companies had strong unions. He wanted significant exposure to human resource management within the union shop configuration with its contract requirements. negotiations and grievances. His netliving practices paid off. Richard landed a human resource position at the new corporate headquarters of a company which had both plant and office unions. This setting provided a double barreled dose of negotiating with unions.

On the evening of Richard's last day at IBM, several of his managers broke one of the then cardinal rules of the firm. They took Richard out drinking and a pub near the office. There were speeches and toasts and much partying. Consequently he arrived home in the wee hours of the morning. The worst part about it was he had to begin his new position the next morning.

At 8:00 a.m. sharp he was in his new boss' office with a large hangover. He was experiencing a strange phenomena. He felt like the whole room was shaking at it seemed like five minute intervals. From the look on his face the boss knew there was something wrong. Finally, Richard said something.

"Pardon me but I have spent four years in the navy and have hung a few benders in that time, but I have never had a hangover like this. It feels like this whole office is shaking." He went on to say, "What really makes it strange is that it is intermittent." He continued, "It only shakes for a few seconds every five minutes."

His boss could not hold back his glee any longer. He said, "We are next to a drop forge operation and when the twenty ton forge drops it actually causes this building to shake." Richard's new boss was a former external auditor from what used to be a "Big Eight" accounting firm. He took a strong liking to Richard and became his mentor immediately. He shared many insights into the business world. For example, he made it clear from day one that he expected Richard to be prepared when he came to see him with a problem that he had at least one viable solution to that problem. Otherwise he said, "I don't need you if I have to solve all your problems for you."

When they moved to the brand new building they spent many long hours in his boss' thirty-sixth floor executive office resulting in valuable lessons learned. He had a knack for stretching Richard's abilities as far as they would go. He brought out talents that even he did not know he possessed.

Many people in the firm were deathly afraid of this particular executive, but Richard was not one of them He always treated Richard with great respect and was kind to him throughout their years together. In fact, after they went their separate ways, they continued to meet occasionally for lunch. He took great pride in Richard's future accomplishments.

As the years passed Richard would use his netliving skills again and again to move to higher positions and earn more responsibility with three other major corporations. He never forgot the secrets his father's HR friend had taught him; first look at the industry and then pick the strongest corporation within that industry. Another lesson Richard learned was to always help other people along the career journey.

Richard and another member of his college class were selected by the president of their university to establish an "alumni career network." Following a year marked by phone calls and meetings, they held a grand kick-off with fifty volunteer alumni present. The group was asked to make themselves available for interviews with graduating seniors. The program got off the ground with a bang and the new Placement Director was pleased at the number of generous volunteers and the number of students taking advantage of this program.

Richard, of course, volunteered to be a member of his alma mater's alumni career network. Over the years he interviewed and gave advice to hundreds of young students who were trying to find their way along life's winding trails. In addition to the young seniors, Richard was contacted by many older alumni who had lost their positions as a result of downsizing and reorganizations. He taught these perplexed people the techniques of netliving he had learned along the way.

Later, while studying for his MBA, Richard decided to write his thesis on "Planning for an Aging Workforce." He spent much time in the library researching the subject area. He studied the then recently enacted changes to the Age Discrimination in Employment Act (ADEA) of 1967, which set the mandatory retirement age for most workers in private industry at seventy years. This was subsequently amended, and there is now no age limitation.

Richard found that although age sixty-five was introduced into this country as the age for retirement, it took on added significance with the Social Security Act of 1935. This decision to base the retirement age on a fixed chronological age, applicable to a wide variety of jobs, was made by a small group of New Deal experts who had been given the task of drafting the now famous bill. This decision was made during the depths of the Great Depression, when almost twenty-five percent of the workforce was unemployed. One of the aims of the legislation was to remove some older workers from the payroll and allow younger workers to take their place while the former received retirement benefits. It is debatable whether Congress in 1935 was fully aware of the social implications of the legislation and the giant step they were taking toward institutionalizing retirement. This legislation had a profound influence on public attitude toward the retired individual.

The more Richard studied the subject, the more interested he became. He found that the real impact of retirement at age sixty-five resulted from the development of private pension plans. These came into popularity, beginning with executives during World War II, when wage controls and excess profit taxes made pensions an attractive alternative to pay increases. Following World War II, private pension plans spread quickly to blue-collar workers. Age sixty-five, the social security starting point, became the age normally used in setting up these private pension programs.

During this intensive time of studying for his masters degree and the work on the thesis, Richard became an advocate for Older Workers. He had become acquainted with many individuals who felt the same way, and they formed a group called "New Careers for Older Americans" that was funded by the Federation for Community Planning. This advocacy group's main thrust was to dispel the myth that older workers are too slow and can't keep up with modern technology.

The group pointed out that several studies have compared order workers with younger ones. Generally, older workers are considered more loyal and more stable in the work force. They have higher skills, fewer accidents and better attendance records. In two surveys about decision-making, older managers required more time to reach decisions but proved more accurate in appraising new information.

Richard's and his colleagues' goal was to help convince the public that older Americans must come to be regarded as potential resources rather than dependent persons; they are part of the solution to this country's economic woes, not part of its problems.

Based on his reputation on the subject of older workers, Richard was asked to speak at several conferences and went on a dozen speaking assignments. He was asked to join the local Council on Older Persons and the National Council on the Aging, Inc. Richard delivered a speech at their national convention in New Orleans, and was honored to be featured on the front page of the morning paper.

Any time he spoke to a group of people about the subject of older workers, he reminded them that we are all members of the same body of society.

Richard was nominated to serve on the Board of Trustees of the local chapter of the Society of Human Resource Management and was elected to serve a three-year term. During that three year period he was Vice President for college relations. He also was in charge of setting up the biannual training classes for those members who wished to take the certification exams. In addition, he was very active in encouraging corporate sponsorship of an all-African American high school in a distressed neighborhood.

For Richard's efforts with the careers of older Americans and the careers of young college graduates, he was awarded the highest honor his alma mater bestows on alumni, the "Alumni Medal." The following year he was awarded "Outstanding Member" by his professional Human Resource Society.

During his acceptance speech for the outstanding member award, Richard related the story of his father's HR friend and how much his taking the time that Saturday morning many years ago had helped him in his chosen career. So he thanked him and his parents whom he felt were smiling down on him from heaven.

NETLIVING NOTES:

* Netliving will help your career development. I've learned that I cannot do it alone.
* Netliving will improve your understanding of business. I've learned that I will see when I am prepared to see.
* Netliving will enhance your social consciousness. I've learned that we are responsible for what we do, no matter how we feel.

CHAPTER SEVEN

PEOPLEHOOD VS PRIESTHOOD

"Success in life has nothing to do with what you gain in life or accomplish for yourself. It's what you do for others."

Danny Thomas (1912-1991)

Growing up in a religious family, Roberta was taught to have the greatest respect for the clergy. She and her brother were taken to church every Sunday for Mass. They attended religion classes one night a week at the direction of their parents. As she grew older and progressed through elementary school, junior high, senior high and college, Roberta continued to grow spiritually.

While she was away at college, she made some solid friendships with students of similar backgrounds. These new relationships reinforced the religious principles she had been taught from early childhood. In addition, the priest at the campus ministry was a positive influence on her and her college friends.

Following graduation, Roberta had difficulty finding the same comfortable atmosphere in the local churches. The priest at her local parish was "from the old school" and spoke of a damning and fearful God. Roberta went looking for a new parish to attend.

For a whole year she went from church to church in search of a "kinder, gentler" atmosphere in which to worship. She asked fellow workers at her new organization if they had any suggestions and pursued their leads. Subconsciously Roberta was looking for the type of sharing church that she had experienced on her college campus.

She had long discussions with her brother Richard on the subject. She would ask him, "What do you think about the homilies in your local church?" She continued, "Are these sermons thought provoking and do they challenge you to be a better person?" Richard had had the same experience since they had attended the same university at different time periods. He felt the same missing comfort level.

Unfortunately, due to the drop in vocations to the priesthood, there were not many young priests being ordained and the older priests were tired from overwork. With the shortage of religious leaders, both priests and nuns, the lay-people were recruited into action. At first this new involvement of ordinary churchgoers in the running of the parish was limited to administrative activity. They conducted fund raising drives in addition to the usual bingo games and card parties. Then they became involved in the actual financial planning of the budget and began to have a voice in how the parish collection was spent.

The balance of power was shifting from the formal approach of a pastor as the sole authority figure to the sharing approach of individual members sharing their abilities as well as their spirituality.

As Roberta became involved in this sharing process, she was amazed at the parallel circumstances taking place in the work world. This netliving among parishioners to strengthen the parishes was also taking place in the workplace with employee involvement and the diminishing role of the authoritative manager. Being a human resource professional, this was an area she wanted to understand and master.

She joined the church council and became active in different committees to help with the business management of the parish while also sharing her spirituality. Roberta was interested in educating the younger members of the parish and promoting the development of their social skills.

Roberta felt strongly that spirituality was a netliving system wherein people approaching people was much more acceptable than the formal authoritative approach of the past. She was determined to promote the team concept of sharing to its greatest potential in both her religious and work arenas.

Her parish was made up of more than two thousand families and was spread over a large geographic area. Roberta devised a plan to bring the parishioners closer together as a group. She proposed to divide the parish into zones, each of which would be represented by a coordinator. These smaller areas would form study groups which would meet weekly to discuss spiritual subjects and to get to know each other.

The other members of the council liked the idea and decided to approach the pastor with the concept. Roberta made the successful presentation. Impressed with the notion, the pastor decided it should be implemented as soon as possible.

Using her netliving experience, Roberta made many phone calls and put a team together to help her communicate this new program to the rest of the parish. Announcements were made from the pulpit and articles appeared in the Sunday bulletin. The response was overwhelming, and there was a strong feeling that the people of the parish had been waiting for such an idea. Of the two thousand families, fifteen hundred signed up to participate -- the best response the parish had ever received to any program they had proposed.

Roberta was excited about the "Sharing" program and put all her extra energy into making it a success. She joined one of the groups that was typical of the others. There were ten members in their circle. Two couples were in their mid-fifties. An older gentleman who had been a valet to a rich and distinguished industrialist also joined the group, along with two younger couples raising teenagers. Meetings were held weekly at each others' homes. The host or hostess would supply coffee and some sort of treat.

One of the young husbands made it clear that his evening would be incomplete without chocolate milk. This became a joke for the group, and a constant at every meeting was a half-gallon of chocolate milk. The oldest member of the group baked a delicious chocolate cake which also became a favorite treat.

The atmosphere at the meetings was informal and friendly. The group started with a prayer, then the leader for that night introduced a subject to be discussed. Lively, interesting discussions brought out some strong convictions. One evening the topic of discussion was abortion and one of the wives of the two young couples, who was a registered nurse, became emotionally upset when she related what the result of a late term abortion looked like. "There was no doubt in my mind," she said, "that fetus was a living person," she continued, "You could count every finger and toe, and they were all there." In her mind there was no doubt the doctor who performed the operation was committing murder.

The following week the topic was more positive. It was the practice of meditation. Roberta gave a brief description of her preparation and practice of meditating. She stated, "First I found a nice comfortable place to perform my meditation," she continued, "Then I turned on a soft, smooth CD that usually had the sound of waves crashing on a beach. This makes me think of one of my favorite beaches," she continued. "Then I began repeating two phrases over and over again -- a mantra, 'Let Go, and Let God.' I would continue this for about half an hour and many wonderful thoughts and insights would come into my mind."

After a short period of time the group became genuine friends and were affectionate with each other. The men shook hands and men and women exchanged hugs at the beginning and end of each meeting.

This group activity made it comfortable for newcomers like Robert, who found it nice to see a friendly face in church on Sunday. As the group continued to meet, they selected books to read, study and discuss. This procedure was educational and helped the group grow closer and more spiritual.

Roberta was also involved in a new program she had suggested for the manufacturing plant where she had the human resources responsibility. Her program carried the simple title of "team concept." Her definition of a team: two or more interdependent individuals synchronized together with direction, utilizing their abilities to achieve individual and common goals.

In her workplace, Roberta found the approach was evolutionary rather than revolutionary, so she chose one production line to introduce this concept. She reasoned that she would use this line as a "pilot" line, and when it was successful, she would then roll out the concept to all the other production lines.

The team planned the work and performed it, managing many of the things supervision or management used to. They met daily to identify, analyze, and solve problems. They scheduled, set goals, gave performance feedback, and hired and fired when necessary. As the team matured in its skills, its duties grew accordingly.

Before embarking on such a huge project, Roberta conducted extensive netliving with her colleagues to establish benchmarks and hopefully find a model. Much to her surprise, there were few business firms in the city which had undertaken this type of program. She was a pioneer in her area.

At the public library Roberta checked out as many books as she could carry on the subjects of quality circles and self-directed work teams. She then spent the next few weeks studying different approaches and came up with her own refined version.

Richard, who was part of Roberta's network, and was very interested in the subject since he was also in the human resource field, had found an article in his local newspaper that he faxed to Roberta. The article entitled "What We Can Learn From Geese." appeared in Ann Landers Advice column from a reader in Ithaca, New York and was published in the Cleveland Plain Dealer, Saturday, August 1, 1998.

Fact No. 1: As each bird flaps its wings, it creates an uplift draft for the bird following. By flying in a "V" formation, the whole flock has a greater flying range than if one bird flew alone.

Lesson No.1: People who share a common direction and sense of community can get where they're going quicker and more easily because they are traveling on the strength of one another.

Fact No. 2: Whenever a goose falls out of formation, it suddenly feels the drag and resistance of trying to fly alone and quickly gets back into formation to take advantage of the lifting power of the bird immediately in front.

Lesson No. 2: If we have as much sense as geese, we will stay in formation and be willing to accept help when we need it and give help when it is needed.

Fact No. 3: When the lead goose gets tired, it rotates back into the formation, and another goose flies in the point position.

Lesson No. 3: Geese instinctively share the task of leadership and do not resent the leader.

Fact No. 4: The geese in formation honk from behind to encourage those up front to keep up their speed.

Lesson No. 4: We need to make sure our honking from behind is encouraging and not something else.

Fact No. 5: When a goose gets sick, is wounded or is shot down, two geese drop out of formation and follow it down to earth to help and protect it. They stay with their disabled companion until it is able to fly again or dies. They then launch out on their own or with another formation or catch up with the flock.

Lesson No. 5: If we have as much sense as geese, we, too, will stand by one another in difficult times and help the one who has dropped out regain his place in the formation.

Roberta was impressed by this piece of wisdom and after thanking her brother, placed it in her team concept training folder with the intention of using it in the near future.

One of the first things the new team agreed to do was to alter their uniforms to give them a distinctive look. Since this workplace was a frozen food plant, all employees had to wear uniforms. Each function required a different color uniform. For example, maintenance mechanics wore green uniforms, sanitation workers wore gray uniforms, and all production employees wore white uniforms with the same colored hair net.

Roberta was appointed the overall coordinator of the program. She insisted her idea was more than a program and worried that the word "program" might be interpreted as a one-shot deal. That was not what she had in mind. She expected this concept to work so well that it would be implemented not only on all the other lines in her plant, but in all the other plants operated by the company.

Many training tasks needed to be performed to make the team operate efficiently. Members had to be cross trained so that each person could perform multiple tasks. In addition, they were accountable for production, quality, costs and schedules. Some team members interviewed and hired new employees, prepared and reviewed team member's performance, made minor repairs, monitored statistical process control and coordinated with other supply departments.

Roberta trained the initial key members in interpersonal skills, which required four vital steps: communication, feedback, problem-solving and decision making. Once the initial crew successfully completed Roberta's training procedure, they trained the new members. The team was constantly encouraged to increase skills, improve the product and solve problems. Roberta's plant manager was fond of saying, "Listen for problems and hear opportunities." This upbeat attitude set a positive tone throughout the plant.

The team concept was not a completely new idea; the Japanese had been using similar productive concepts since the end of W.W.II. It was, however, new for this plant and some of the old time managers were concerned about their job security. They felt threatened and were unsure about the need for their services, wondering if they would be on the "outside looking in."

Roberta took the responsibility to teach the managers and supervisors that they must change the way they traditionally led employees. This was very difficult for some because their leadership techniques had been developed in traditional settings over long periods of time. The leaders who successfully made the transition found it exciting, personally satisfying, and well worth the initial frustration and confusion.

Roberta had to convince the managers and supervisors of the need to become skilled at empowering their employees by turning over power, information, knowledge, skills and decisions to others. She persuaded them to become skilled teachers, counselors and coaches who were excited by other people's learning and growing activities. She led them to see themselves as facilitators and to become almost totally people-oriented. The managers and supervisors learned that most of their time would be spent removing barriers across departments and giving attention to functions that hindered workers' performances.

She taught them how to improve their listening skills instead of just telling people what to do. On the spot decisions would have to be made instead of passing the question up the line. She stressed the urgent need to be a good role model and motivator.

The first year review of this concept was encouraging. All the numbers were favorable for production, quality, down time, ingredient costs and equipment repair costs. The plant manager was pleased and decided to expand the concept to all the other production lines in the plant.

Roberta moved the people from the trial production line and used them to start the team concept on all the other lines. They proved be the best leaders the plant had ever seen. Overall output and quality for the entire plant improved by twenty-five percent in the first year of operation. Eventually the concept was spread over the entire corporation, and its application greatly enhanced performance and bottom line numbers.

As a result of this great success, Roberta was promoted to the corporate headquarters and assigned to be in charge of all the human resource functions at that location. As is the case with any change in an organization's culture, there were many who were pleased with the opportunity to use their brain-power more; they enjoyed the feeling of being a part of the team. On the other hand, there were employees who resisted change despite the hard evidence of positive results.

Roberta was pleased that her company's leadership committed to the primary idea that each and every person in the workplace was valuable. Every worker, regardless of their level in the organization was a resource, and everyone was capable of constantly learning to improve themselves, their work and the overall performance of the organization.

While Roberta was involved in implementing the team concept program and insuring it worked smoothly, her private life suffered. One evening at the parish circle meeting, an older member of the group asked if she had a special young man. When she indicated she did not, all kinds of helpful hints came forth based on memories and past experience -- yet another netliving example. She was told of a recent college graduate from an out-of-town women's college who returned home to find most of her high school girlfriends had already married and were busy raising families. Roberta could relate to this enterprising young lady who had contacted the bishop's office and received permission to set up a weekly dance that would be a meeting place for all recent college graduates. Admittance to the dance simply required the graduate to show an identification card from his or her college.

After hearing about this idea, Roberta could not wait to get started on her advanced version of the "dance connection." She talked it over with her parish pastor to make sure he did not see any problems with this novel approach. With his blessing, she contacted the church diocesan office to get the names of contacts in the various parishes throughout the city and to inform the authorities that such a program was being organized.

Although her brother Richard was already married, he and his wife felt it was a good idea so they helped with the phone calls. Many were made and Roberta used all her netliving skills to put a core group together to plan and implement this attempt at getting young people together. All the people she talked to thought it was a great idea and were willing to do their share of the planning and follow-through on implementing their program.

One friend knew of a hall which could be rented at a reasonable cost. She was given the assignment to make the contact. Another friend knew of a disc jockey willing to volunteer his time and talent for the foreseeable future. A group was assigned to design a flyer and make sure it was published in all the church bulletins throughout the diocese.

Roberta was pleased with the enthusiasm displayed by her committee and was anxious about many things the day before the first dance. "What if no one comes?," she worried. "What if they don't like the music? What if they don't like the hall?" All these questions ran through her brain as she tried to dress for the big event.

At eight p.m., a sell-out crowd jammed the dance hall. The music was loud enough and the variety of tunes was acceptable. Roberta received many accolades for her great idea. The dances continued every Saturday night for many years. Couples throughout the city met at these alumni dances. The netliving and peoplehood were in contrast with the formal structure of the church with the clerical hierarchy running everything, but this in no way suggested that the priesthood or formal religion was unimportant to the society.

This was also true of the management structure in Roberta's working environment. The managers and supervisors were important in the "team concept" approach, but their roles had changed just like the role of the pastor of the local church.

NETLIVING NOTES:

* Netliving will help your peoplehood skills. I've learned that two people can look at the exact same thing and see something totally different.
* Netliving will enhance your team building ability. I've learned that it takes years to build up trust, and only seconds to destroy it.
* Netliving will improve your social circle. I've learned that we don't have to change friends if we understand that friends change.

OLD LIFE PLANNING MODEL

Figure 8-1

FIGURE 8-2

NEW LIFE PLANNING MODEL

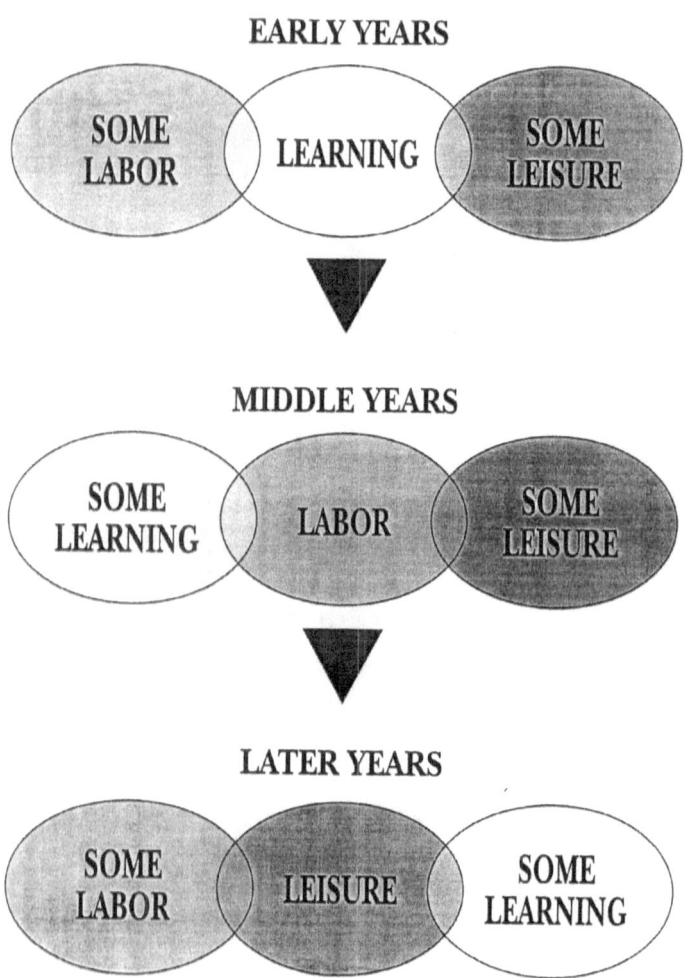

Figure 8-2

CHAPTER EIGHT

TO LIFELONG LEARNING

"We should so live and labor in our times that what came to us as seed may go to the next generation as blossom, and what came to us as blossom may go to them as fruit. This expresses the true spirit in the love of mankind."

Henry Ward Beecher (1813 - 1887)

By the time Richard reached his mid-twenties, he was convinced that his body and mental ability had ceased to grow. He noticed certain abilities had begun to decline, such as how quickly he could learn new things. When he read about this phenomena in one of his sociology classes it caused him concern. But as he continued to study he found that other aspects of his "total self" were still growing. He learned that he could mature throughout life in the areas of wisdom, perspective, and satisfaction. Such lifelong growth is determined by the cultivation of interests. He became aware that, provided he focused his energies and was resourceful, he could benefit by netliving with others. The old Life Planning Model was linear (See Figure 8-1) and Richard felt he wanted to pursue the new Life Planning Model (See Figure 8-2.)

Richard decided while still in college that he wanted to remain mentally alert and in touch with the world around him. He felt he could better meet life's challenges and understand it and himself by staying on top of current events. He also knew he wanted to be mentally well-rounded and have a broad understanding in a wide range of subjects.

This view was consistent with the mission of the Jesuit university Richard was attending. At a Jesuit college or university, the presence of Jesuits and others inspired by the vision of Saint Ignatius Loyola, founder of the Society of Jesus in the year 1540, is of paramount importance. This vision, which reflects the value system of the Gospels, is expressed in the SPIRITUAL EXERCISES OF SAINT IGNATIUS, the source of Jesuit life and activity.

Richard learned that the Jesuit spirit brings to education a rationality appropriately balanced by human affection, an esteem for the individual as a unique person, training in discerning choices, openness to change, and a quest for God's greater glory in the use of his world's goods. Richard experienced that the EXERCISES promotes justice by affirming the equal dignity of all persons and seeks balance between reliance on divine assistance and natural capacities. The effort to combine faith and culture takes on different forms at different times in Jesuit universities. Innovation, experimentation, and training for social leadership are essential to the Jesuit tradition.

The educational system Richard experienced provided opportunities for him to develop as a total human person. He was well grounded in liberalizing, humanizing arts and sciences; proficient in the skills that lead to clear, persuasive expression, and trained in the intellectual discipline necessary to pursue a subject in depth. He was made aware of the interrelationship of all knowledge and the need for integration and synthesis.

Richard was able to commit to a tested scale of values and to demonstrate the self-discipline necessary to live by those values. Alert to learning as a life-long process, he was open to change as he matured, respectful of his own culture and that of others. He was aware of the interdependence of all humanity and sensitive to the need of social justice in response to current social pressures and problems.

As Richard discovered, school is where interests may be aroused and cultivated. His resourcefulness allowed him to develop his interests that were fostered in education. He was fortunate that his high school was not so conscious of examinations and grades that it stifled the awakening of individual interests within him.

His sense of wonder, curiosity and delight came from the enjoyment of learning and the development of skills. This process was enhanced because the learning or the skill was not constantly measured and tested. Richard did not feel pressured to achieve. His high school was considered progressive because it emphasized enjoyment and self-directed "discovery" learning.

While studying anthropology in his senior year at college, Richard found the full-time students comprise a substantial minority among young adults throughout the developed world. In Britain, twenty percent of those aged eighteen to twenty one are students, and in the U.S. the figure is only slightly higher. Even in countries where students are less numerous, they are an extremely important sector of the population. He found that students attending institutions of higher education are in a position to develop a wide range of interests. Time, opportunity and external encouragement help them develop resourcefulness. This is true not only of their academic work, but of all their time and activities.

This traditional ideal of a student's life allows for the development of ideas through netliving marked by informal discussions with staff and fellow students. Richard was free to explore new areas as well as special academic subjects. The wider fields of religion, politics, sex, emotion, the arts, social issues, etc., continued to intrigue him. He also had a continuing interest in developing his body. Putting this interest into action, he pursued competence in sports and yoga.

One of the problems that Richard encountered while in college was the isolation of universities from the world of politics and public affairs. He had lacked the opportunities to test his abstract ideas in the "real world." To remedy this, Richard took a summer job in the human resource area as a benefits clerk. He joined that ranks of students who sought employment during their university years. Working one's way through college had been common in America for a long time, and the trend continued to grow. A recent survey report done by the College Placement Council shows that seventy five percent of college students hold summer jobs to earn tuition and gain experience.

Working in the human resource department of a manufacturing plant gave Richard an opportunity to pay some of his college expenses. More importantly it gave him an opportunity to gain first hand experience, decide on his career choice and strengthen his resume.

Upon graduation, Richard accepted a position with IBM which had a well-established tuition refund program. Eventually Richard planned to pursue an MBA. The expensive degree would be made possible by the firm's willingness to pay seventy-five per cent of the tuition plus the entire cost of textbooks and course materials.

In the back of his mind, Richard had always wanted to become a college professor. Through netliving he learned that most local four-year colleges would accept a masters degree for adjunct professors. This fact fueled his desire to attend graduate school in a few years. To accomplish his goal he would have to take some business courses to qualify for admission since he had taken all liberal arts courses for his undergraduate degree.

Besides netliving with his sister, Roberta, who had already earned her MBA, Richard also netlived with many of his business associates to determine the best institution of higher learning to approach, and which had a program that would accommodate the full-time worker.

He found such an institution, then wrote out a five-year plan indicating the preparatory courses and the three years of the part-time MBA program. He also factored in the GMAT test preparation.

In a poll conducted by U.S.A. TODAY, people on the street were asked what they would do if they won one million dollars in a contest. Twenty percent stated they would return to school. The main reason many would go back to college is one of the reasons Richard wanted to return. He knew the difference higher education would make in his paycheck. His own sister was living proof of the financial advantage of a graduate degree. Studies done by the Society for Human Resource Management have shown that an executive with an MBA can make as much as $28,000 a year more than the executive without an advanced degree.

Richard knew one of the keys to his success in graduate school would be to netlive with other students and form study teams. Hence he contacted several of the registered students before the formal program began and formed a GMAT study group to prepare for the three-hour examination. He often wished had had done more netliving and team studying while an undergraduate. He was determined not to make the same mistake twice.

One of his best friends in graduate school was an Indian-American student originally from Bombay. They became well balanced study teammates. D.C. as he was affectionately called, was an industrial engineer with an analytical mind. Richard had a liberal arts background and not much experience with numbers.

When it came to analyzing a serious program in a management course, D.C. excelled. Richard took the lead when it came to writing papers. They spent much time together and enjoyed each other's company. Although serious students, they found time to discuss sports and other less important subjects.

D.C. had some difficulty with the social aspects of American society. He came from a culture that considered women inferior to men and it was difficult for him to adjust his thinking. He and Richard held long and often heated discussions about the fair treatment of females in the workplace.

Management style was another subject that caused them some serious disagreements. D.C. was a traditional authoritarian style manager while Richard believed in a participative (team management) style. Many disagreements resulted as they gradually gained a better understanding of each other's perspective.

Richard and D.C. netlived with other members of the class on a regular basis. Each member of the team studied a different aspect of the assignment, which multiplied the effectiveness of each individual team member. This was a grueling time for Richard and his classmates. All of them had full time positions and family responsibilities. The weekly schedules were staggering. Classes met every Friday evening and all day Saturday for a period of twenty-seven months. No breaks or vacations were scheduled into this intensive program. The formula required at least three hours of study for every hour of class, amounting to an additional forty-eight hours weekly from each student's already busy schedule.

By graduation day, Richard and his colleagues were exhausted. Following the ceremony and posing for pictures, they all went out for a dinner celebration. The following week, Richard, his wife and three children began a thirty-day coast to coast trip as a reward for all the time he had spent away from them while studying.

In preparation for the trip, Richard's wife and children did much netliving with friends who had previously made the western trip. They also received travel books and maps from the American Automobile Association of which they were members. The public library provided additional information about places to visit and sites to see. The entire family felt this was a golden opportunity to learn first-hand about this wonderful land we call home.

∞∞∞∞∞∞∞∞∞∞∞∞∞∞∞∞∞∞∞∞∞∞∞∞∞∞∞∞∞∞∞

Richard was reminded of the many learning experiences he had been exposed to during his four years of service in the navy. He had enlisted while a senior in high school and went off to boot camp the following October. He joined the service partly because of the three-fold learning experience offered. First he was to learn the electronics trade as a high speed radio operator. Secondly, by traveling from country to country, he would be exposed to various cultures and people throughout the world. Thirdly he would be eligible for the Korea War Veteran's GI Bill which, among other things, would help pay for a four-year college degree.

As a native of a small Pennsylvania town, taking his first train ride from Pittsburgh to the U.S. Naval Training facility at Bainbridge, Maryland, was a large scale adventure and a primary learning experience. The eighteen-year-old had previously never traveled outside of the greater Pittsburgh area.

After four months in boot camp Richard was selected and enrolled in Class A Radio School also at the Bainbridge Naval base. During the intensive six month training period, he learned about Ohm's Law and many other electronic theories and principles. Besides learning about radio and electronics, Richard and his fellow sailors planned road trips to various cities surrounding the base.

One classmate, who shared Richard's last name, made his home in nearby Philadelphia. He took Richard home with him on weekends and they explored the "City of Brotherly Love." They enjoyed Irish dances on Saturday nights. They danced and drank beer 'till the wee hours of the morning. On Sundays Richard and his Philly friend went to church with the family. A large city such as Philadelphia provided a wonderful learning experience for a young man from a small town. Richard took full advantage of the opportunities offered, such as Sunday afternoon visits to historic sites. The "Liberty Bell" at Independence Hall was a favorite spot. Other weekends the two sailors would venture into Baltimore with other classmates to discover what that city had to offer.

Richard shared a funny story regarding how these two friends met. On the first day of class in radio school they fell out in front of the barracks for a "Muster" or to a civilian it would be a role call. As the big salty chief called out the names in alphabetic order there was what sounded like an echo when he called out "Dolan." He tried it again and there it was two people yelling "here." The burly chief petty officer boatswain mate did not think this was funny and began to get steamed. He called out "Dolan" the third time and the echo continued. He said, "Dolan, front and center." That is when Richard met Joe Dolan. They have been best friends ever since.

Finally, Richard traveled to Washington D.C. to visit his twin sister, Roberta, who was living there with her husband. It was a great learning experience to tour the impressive historic sites in the D.C. area. The Smithsonian was Richard's favorite museum in Washington. He, his sister and brother-in-law spent many interesting hours there.

These weekend trips were fun and educational. Richard planned several other trips including one to see Annapolis. He was deeply impressed by the history stored at this beautiful location. He spent hours walking the same grounds that the famous naval heroes had walked many years before.

With radio school completed, Richard was assigned to an aircraft carrier stationed in Norfolk, Virginia. The USS KULA GULF, nicknamed a "jeep" carrier, was a converted tanker on which the Kaiser company (who also manufactured Jeeps) had installed flight decks with elevators to accommodate aircraft. Only a few yards longer than a football field, the converted warship was considerably shorter than a normal aircraft carrier.

Following his year aboard the KULA GULF, which was named for a famous battle in the South Pacific, Richard received orders to transfer to North Africa. The base was located in what was then know as French Morocco in a little desert town called Sidi Iyia. The Communication Center for classified information, located below ground, was the direct link between Washington D.C. and the Sixth Fleet operating in the Mediterranean Sea. There was also a navy air base about twenty miles away at what was then called Port Lyautie.

Richard entered a state of shock when he received these orders. Africa, with its lions and tigers and all those threatening natives, was a scary thought for him. But orders are orders and he accepted the intimidating transfer with his guard up. He was pleasantly surprised when he finally arrived in Africa. Richard saw no lions or tigers and the natives were not as belligerent as he had anticipated. The navy had a private beach on the Atlantic Ocean and the climate was similar to Arizona's. The temperatures were often in the nineties, but it was a dry heat and not as stifling as might be expected. Two months of rain were offset by the other ten months, which were bright and sunny. An added attraction was that it was "French" Morocco and the sailors loved to watch the young French ladies nonchalantly changing their clothes, getting ready for the beach. That was a real learning experience.

The day Richard's troop ship arrived in Casablanca, the restless natives were fighting for their independence. When he boarded the navy bus for the trip to the base, he noticed a machine gun mounted on the escort jeep manned by two formidable-looking marines. The sailors received a quick orientation on survival in a land at war.

Upon arrival at the base, Richard was informed that he was restricted to the base and that he was assigned to a B.A.R. team, which meant he would have to learn to operate a Browning Automatic Rifle. Some of the natives were trying to infiltrate the base and Richard would be part of a team that was to shoot them as they attempted to crawl over the barbed wire fence.

"Wait a minute," Richard exclaimed! "If I wanted to be a shooter I would have joined the army." That did little to remedy the situation, so he spent many hours learning how to efficiently fire his BAR, and then many dark nights hoping that there would not be a native foolish enough to try to scale the fence during his watch.

The revolution subsided by the beginning of the summer months. Richard began to plan for a thirty-day leave to be spent touring the British Isles and Spain. Using his netliving skills, he arranged to meet his aunt and uncle in London. The Pennsylvania couple volunteered to be his tour guides throughout England, Ireland, Scotland and Wales. Richard was excited at the chance to explore his family's roots.

Through further netliving, Richard located a former high school chum, also stationed in North Africa, who was coincidentally flying on the same aircraft to Madrid and London. The two old friends had a wonderful time visiting the various historic sites in Madrid, using their faltering high school Spanish. Richard was amazed at the rate of speed with which the natives spoke and had difficulty understanding them. But languages skills were not necessary to enjoy photographing the beauty of Spain.

After an overnight visit to Madrid they boarded another military transport plane from the airbase and were on their way to London. Both had studied the travel brochures of historic attractions and they were thrilled with anticipation. They landed at famous Heathrow airport and cleared customs. It was a typical rainy London day when they took a cab to their hotel.

Driving on the left side of the street was unsettling at first, but the sailors became accustomed to it quickly. Their Cockney cabby brought them up to speed on the current situation in the city. Enroute to their hotel, they passed the famous Tower of

London and the London Bridge. They stood in awe at many sights they had only seen in books or on the large and small screens back home.

That evening, after checking in and freshening up, they headed out to "hit the town." In conversing with their fellow sailors back at the base, they were encouraged to take in "Piccadilly Circus." Richard, still the rural hayseed, thought he was going to see clowns and elephants. Instead, Richard and his hometown friend were amazed at the beautiful young women walking along the street. One of these beauties grabbed Richard's classmate, opened up the fly of his trousers and began to handle his private parts.

Both sailors were in a state of shock that such a beautiful creature could do such a crude thing. When the woman opened her mouth, nothing but four letter words poured out in a strong London accent. She asked if there were "players" or just "spectators." The shock prevented them from fully understanding what she was saying. When they explained that they were just tourists and not part of the "john trade," she was disgusted and said, "They don't make those Yank sailors like they used to."

The young sailors spent the next few days walking the streets of London, taking in all the tourist sights. They were careful to avoid the "red light" district of Picadilly Circus.

On Monday morning Richard bid farewell to his mate. He headed to the train station to travel to the North of England where he was to meet his aunt and uncle. They met in the city of Durham in Durham County where his father had been raised. Both Richard's mother and father had been born in Ireland and had emigrated, with their respective families, to England to obtain employment.

Richard's father's family had settled into the small coal mining town of Kelloe in Durham County. His paternal grandfather had been a coal miner and all of his sons had followed him into the mines. Richard was thrilled to see the actual home where his father had been raised. All of his relatives came out to meet the "bonnie Yank sailor." They held parties and sing-a-longs. Many smiling Irish faces sang the sad Irish ballads.

Next, Richard's aunt and uncle took him to visit his mother's home in Cumberland County on the border of Scotland. The little hamlet where she had been raised was called Cleator Moore. It was a mining community, but copper was the product instead of coal. Her relatives greeted Richard with the same zeal as his paternal relatives. They had a grand time and took the "Yank" to see all the sights around his mother's childhood home. He was getting good use of his second-hand 35 millimeter camera. Great photo opportunities abounded everywhere Richard looked. He wanted to document as much as possible to show his parents and especially his twin sister.

The threesome boarded a train in Cumberland County and headed to Hollyhead in Wales to meet a ferryboat that would carry them across the Irish Sea to Dublin. This was a magical trip for Richard. From the time he was a small boy he had heard the stories about the Irish Sea and the vivid green of the "Old Sod." When they approached the island home of his ancestors, he became all choked up at the sight of the emerald green grass that came all the way down to meet the sea.

The next three weeks were spent touring the famous landmarks of Ireland. In Dublin, Richard met relatives from his aunt's side of the family. Some of the younger family members joined Richard on his tour of their city. They proudly showed him Connel's Bridge and many other landmarks along the River Liffy. As a beer drinker, he was especially interested in the Guinness Brewery.

They visited his mother's home county of Wicklow and his father's Sligo County. Richard's aunt was from County Mayo, so they spent most of the three remaining weeks using her stepmother's authentic Irish Cottage (thatched roof and all) as a stepping-off point. Every day they ventured out to visit different areas of the country and every evening gathered around the fireplace singing until the wee hours. It was a great learning experience for Richard and the memories would enrich the rest of his life.

Getting back to Richard's family's "Western trip," as it became know in the immediate family group, all the preparations had been made. The family had decided to follow the central route across Route 80 through the heartland to the Pacific. They would return via the southern Route 70. These interstate highways provided good reliable roads with plenty of motels, restaurants and gas stations.

For the next thirty days, Richard and his family netlived their way across the U.S. In Salt Lake City, where Richard attended a three-day Human Resource Convention, they netlived with some good friends who lived in nearby Bountiful.

A three-day stop in Sacramento, at the home of Richard's wife's former student, was a welcome break from motels. The beautiful sprawling ranch with its swimming pool was especially popular with Richard's children.

After three days of living in paradise, Richard and his wife had some difficulty extracting their children from this ideal setting. Back on the road, they moved up and down the coast of California, taking in the redwood forests and beautiful beaches along the mighty Pacific Ocean.

Their ride across the desert in the middle of the night was a highlight of the trip. The breath-taking view of the Grand Canyon from the southern rim gave Richard goose bumps, upon encountering the magnificent vastness of the canyon.

The remainder of the trip home passed rather quickly. Since there had not been any rainfall in the western states for an entire month and the daily temperature hovered around one hundred degrees, the sight-seeing stops became less and less frequent. They did take time to visit the Merrimac Cave in Missouri and were delighted by the formations they discovered. The cool temperature inside the cave was refreshing relief from the sweltering world on the surface.

Later that summer Richard did some netliving with one of his former MBA classmates who was teaching at a women's weekend college. Richard landed a part-time teaching assignment for an overview course on human resource management. The weekend schedule worked well for Richard since he was still working his full-time human resource position.

When his alma mater became aware of his moonlighting, they recruited him for their business school as an adjunct professor. He continued teaching for the next twelve years. One of the many things Richard learned from his teaching experience was that the best way to learn a subject was by teaching the subject to others.

As time passed, Richard became interested in attending pre-retirement seminars offered by his company and some financial institutions. He became proficient in various areas of concern.

NETLIVING NOTES:

* Netliving will enhance your lifelong learning. I've learned that when the student is ready the teacher will appear.
* Netliving will help you to learn from your travel experiences. I've learned more from being there than from any book or magazine.
* Netliving will facilitate your travel planning. I've learned from friends and relatives who have "been there and done that."

FIGURE 9-1

Figure 9-1

CHAPTER NINE

FOR EMOTIONAL BALANCE

"We should strive to understand the weakness of others."

Ellen G. White (1827-1915)

From an early age Roberta heard that moderation is the secret to a successful and balanced life. These words of wisdom were echoed throughout her childhood and in her young adult years when her parents and grandparents had a chance to talk to her about the secrets of life.

As an adult, and especially in her career as a professional human resource manager, she became involved in many emotionally charged situations that required rational balance. On one such occasion, Roberta was approached by a cook from the plant with a troubled look on her face. Invited into the privacy of Roberta's office, the long-service employee burst into tears approaching hysteria.

Roberta calmed the cook and offered her a tissue; the sad story began to unfold. This employee had unfortunately married at a young age, to a street person who was fond of a lifestyle that included excessive drinking and gambling. Later she learned he was also a drug addict. These burdens, coupled with the fact that he was unemployed, naturally led to many severe domestic squabbles.

As the story gradually unraveled, Roberta heard how the husband had borrowed money from a "loan shark," gotten in debt far over his head and failed to pay back the money at the required time. The loan shark had broken through the front door of their home at three a.m. that morning armed with a sawed-off shotgun demanding the money.

The employee trembled visibly as she related these events of the early morning encounter while Roberta listened carefully, wondering, What can I do for this poor, frightened person? After a few moments, Roberta decided to ask the plant manager to grant this loyal employee a pay advance. Obviously this would be an unusually large pay advance, but the circumstances seemed to warrant a try. When she approached the plant manager and told him the whole story, he agreed to arrange to advance the $5,000 without blinking an eye. He knew the woman well and felt it was a good investment in a loyal employee.

When Roberta conveyed the good news the employee broke down and sobbed with relieved appreciation. One of the conditions that Roberta attached to the loan was that the employee urge her spouse to join Gamblers Anonymous. The employee herself needed support and she joined Alanon.

During subsequent years Roberta and this employee developed a close friendship both at work and off the job too. Many times they would get together to share their thoughts and feelings and from time to time to help each other remain emotionally balanced. Thus, netliving proved to be an effective tool for this employee and her family. Her spouse succeeded in giving up gambling, stopped drinking alcoholic beverages, and overcame his addiction to illegal drugs. He was fortunate indeed to find a steady job and was grateful to Roberta and the company that demonstrated such great faith in and genuine appreciation for his wife.

Shortly after this incident a supervisor came to see Roberta regarding one of his men, a long-time employee who in recent years was beset by a string of emotional problems. Originally his problems were evidenced by intermittent attendance on the job. The supervisor noticed that the employee's attendance pattern indicated he was often absent on Fridays and Mondays. This pattern continued for a six month period. When verbal and written warnings failed, it became obvious to Roberta and the supervisor that this individual had a serious problem and a safe bet was that it concerned alcohol abuse.

When the next phase in the corrective discipline process meant suspension for this individual, Roberta decided to take another approach. She had been trained in counseling alcoholics and drug addicts and she knew the warning signs.

She reviewed the indicated approach with the supervisor and they agreed to meet with the employee and offer the options of either twenty-eight days in "detox" or a three-day suspension that would be the final step before termination. Both Roberta and the supervisor knew that losing a job consequently the source of income that continues to feed the addiction is a major concern for the user.

When they confronted the employee it did not take long to convince him to enter the rehab center and "take the cure." He took the first positive step and admitted he was an alcoholic and needed help. He acknowledged he could not drink like a normal drinker. He knew one drink would lead to a "bender," and he would be absent from work on the next day as he tried to "recover." If the binge was on a Friday he would be on a so called "toot" for the whole weekend, including the following Monday.

His is a great success story. Everyone in the plant was happy for him and his achievement. When he returned to work he looked much healthier and happier. For several years he continued to do well on the Alcoholics Anonymous program by going to meetings and netliving with his sponsor and other members of the group.

Then he began to gain weight. He had switched addictions and gradually went from overdrinking to overeating. After some time one of his fellow AA's mentioned that it was quite common for addicts to switch compulsions. This made him very angry, and that anger was the reason his supervisor was in Roberta's office this morning.

During the last six months the supervisor had noticed that the employee was extremely quiet around his fellow workers. He would not engage in shop-talk with anyone. The fellow he had been closest to previously could not get even a "good morning" from him. In fact, some of his fellow workers expressed strong concern about his mental "balance." They were concerned he might "explode" and they felt it would be a tragic experience if he did.

Roberta and the man's supervisor decided to confront him with the situation and suggest he take a personal leave of absence with pay until he could get himself straightened out. He was relieved when they finally brought the problem out in the open. He admitted he had switched compulsions and felt extremely angry at everyone. He admitted he went home at night and punched a light weight punching bag for hours until exhausted he fell asleep, physically and mentally depleted. He said the inner resentment caused him to pound nails into a board for hours at a time. He was full of rage at himself for going from being a drunk to being a food addict.

The suggestion that he consider joining Overeaters Anonymous was made by Roberta and she also proposed he take a month off to pursue becoming food abstinent. He had heard of the program from being in AA but had never seriously considered it for himself. Both his supervisor and Roberta made it clear that he was not to return to work until he had regained emotional balance in his life.

The troubled employee attended a twelve-step meeting (either OA or AA) for the next thirty days and through the netliving and sharing found in both programs was able to overcome the intense anger he felt for himself. His weight decreased by thirty pounds and he looked much improved physically when he arrived to see Roberta and his supervisor to receive permission to return to work. He convinced them that one day at a time he could be a balanced individual emotionally and that his life was in order.

Increased emotional problems with employees is a sign of the nineties, Roberta noticed. One of the dominant contributing factors is the high stress level caused by both parents working full-time positions and the single parent struggling to do it all alone, producing latch-key children with the guilt and shame that situation generates for the caring parents.

One Monday morning a few months later, Roberta found two terrified female employees waiting for her to arrive at her office. One employee was there as moral support for the other, who had been living with a man for about six months when she began to notice some unusual behavior. Her boyfriend had begun drinking heavily and she suspected he may have started taking illegal drugs.

This particular morning she was so shaken it was difficult for her to control her voice. Her girlfriend did most of the talking. This boyfriend had become abusive to the young woman, and it had culminated over the weekend with physical and mental abuse.

He had punched and kicked her and shouted nasty and vulgar words at her while administering the blows. The final despicable act occurred when the man, knowing her fondness for a pet canary named "chipper," placed the tiny bird in the microwave oven and "nuked" it. If he could do such a thing, it was a fair question to ask what else was he capable of doing.

With this severe situation hanging over the employee's head the problem fell into Roberta's lap. Being experienced in handling domestic situations, Roberta called the local women's shelter hot line and within an hour the three women met with a shelter representative in a public parking lot. The abused employee was advised to file a police report and have the locks changed on her apartment door.

This plan would provide for the abuser to come to the apartment, discover he could not enter, become enraged and break down the door. That act would give the police sufficient grounds to arrest him for breaking and entering. This would buy her some time to get settled in the shelter and find some temporary security.

At the the women's shelter she was given a clean room and much needed emotional support from the staff and other residents. She shared her story and listened to their similar tales of anguish. The most important aspect of this shelter was to convince her that she was not alone. Roberta maintained communications with the employee and her sympathetic friend throughout the ordeal.

Eventually, through counseling and the support of the shelter, the employee decided to become a member of the U.S. Air Force, moving to Texas for basic training. Roberta continued to stay in touch and was happy to know her netliving friend had met a wonderful, gentle and caring individual who eventually became her spouse.

Emotions always ran high during the fall with the arrival of football season. Some employees wore the colors and attire vividly representing their favorite teams. These loyal fans naturally rankled one another with commentary. Most of the time it was good humored bantering, but one Monday morning in October, after a certain team had won an overwhelming victory, the teasing made an ugly "about-face." Two otherwise mature men escalated a loud argument over the game's outcome into a physical confrontation. Here were two highly experienced and valued employees apparently set on jeopardizing their careers with the company over the results of a game of football.

Roberta, caught in the middle of this melee, fought back a grin as these adult gentlemen explained the details of what had happened. They each took their team's fate very seriously and were emotionally involved to the extent that the game became equivalent to being like a member of their respective families. When an outsider said something derogatory about a member of the family, that declaration would of course become "fightin words."

After calming the men down, Roberta indicated the company would issue a written warning that would be noted in their personnel files. Had these two been other than long term employees, and both with prior good work records, they would probably have been terminated. Thus another crisis was overcome and through netliving the word spread throughout the company that sports rivalries had to be contained. Both of these gentlemen ceased flaunting their team's colors and were noticeably subdued in their subsequent discussions of football games.

Netliving played an important role in a much more serious case that involved a female employee, who, when she was a child, was sexually molested by a close member of her family. This traumatic background came to Roberta's attention when fellow workers noticed that the employee was depressed and had isolated herself from others.

During a counseling interview this female employee indicated she had recently become aware, through therapy, that she had been sexually molested when she was a six-year-old child. She indicated to Roberta that she had suppressed the memory of this terrible experience for more than thirty years. However, while talking to the therapist about how dirty she felt, the sad tale came spilling out.

The realization that such a dreadful thing had happened to her at the hands of her mother's forty-year-old brother made her feel that she had done something wrong. A heavy burden of guilt and shame was kept locked inside for all those years. She told Roberta that she could not have a normal relationship with any male because of the suppressed memories.

She realized the reason she used alcohol, consumed food far beyond normal requirements and avoided the use of makeup was to place a wall or barrier around herself so she would not be attractive to men in any way. Roberta listened intently and was supportive and appreciative of the woman's situation and was glad to be made aware of the underlying difficulty. Roberta suggested that in addition to the therapy, the woman might want to consider joining a support group whereby she could netlive with other women who had suffered similar experiences.

Roberta obtained contact information for several such groups and was pleased to learn that the employee successfully joined one of them. She met weekly with Roberta and within a few months there was a noticeable improvement in her behavior and appearance. She was a highly skilled employee and it would have also been a loss to the company to lose her services. Listening for problems and hearing the solutions paid off again.

During this time period Roberta attended a lecture which explained the effect of stress on emotional balance. The speaker provided a simple example. She said that all of us have an internal cauldron which is constantly boiling. It is fueled by little daily stresses -- when you can't find that important piece of paper, when that driver cuts you off in traffic, when you get on the slow line in the grocery store. These are all examples of putting another log on the fire that further heats that boiling pot. All of us experience these everyday annoyances. Usually we handle the major crisis we encounter better than these everyday small things which, when put all together, cause much stress and anxiety (See Figure 9-1).

Coping with this boiling cauldron in your mid-section is a process called venting. You can visualize vents coming out of that pot you have enclosed within yourself and let all that steam blow off through those vents. Some people vent better by talking to someone about what is bothering them (another form of netliving). Others take a nice long walk, some prefer a more strenuous jog and some use "all out" running. Some enjoy sitting down and reading a good book. Others come in touch with their feelings by writing or keeping a journal. Some people meditate and pray for help in overcoming the accumulated stress and they ask for help with their emotional control These are all examples of proactive or positive venting.

There are also negative ways of venting, as Roberta had learned from the broad exposure that comes with the job of being a human resource person in a two-thousand employee plant. Often an individual blows up over a trivial annoyance; the innocent victim is the other person in the wrong place at the wrong time.

Others vent in a destructive manner by abusing substances such as alcohol and drugs to relieve the stress. Unfortunately these addictions only compound the problem and make the stress level even higher over the long run.

Many people turn to other supposedly harmless compulsions such as gambling, overeating and overspending to relieve the stress of everyday life. By stuffing themselves with food they hope to turn down the fire under that pot that boils in their stomachs. To the contrary, such behavior only fuels the flames. Others feel that by hiding themselves in gambling or compulsive shopping the pain will go away. Wrong again; these tactics only make the stress more serious as the resulting economic woes increase.

Roberta could relate to everything the lecturer brought up, and she made notes to incorporate many of the positive suggestions into her daily routine. She planned to use this information to netlive with her co-workers and also with friends outside the company.

The additional netliving lessons she learned about balancing emotions concerned maintaining a balance with the three L's throughout all phases of life: LEARNING, LABOR, AND LEISURE. Netliving had also taught her that those of us who are physically and spiritually fit are better able to control emotions despite the onslaught of stress in our daily lives.

NETLIVING NOTES:

* Netliving and sharing our problems helps us cope with stress. I've learned that a good friend is better than a therapist.
* Netliving will help extinguish some of those flames under the boiling pot. I've learned when I give my problems to God, solutions are on the way.
* Netliving is a powerful tool to help us stay emotionally balanced. I've learned that it's hard to determine where to draw the line between being nice and not hurting people's feelings and standing up for what you believe.

CHAPTER TEN

THE MID-LIFE CRISIS

"It is never too late to be what you might have been."

George Eliot (1819-1880)

As Richard approached his late thirties he began to experience a mid-career crisis. A crisis which, he later found out, was only a part of the even greater crisis popularized by Gail Sheehey in her book, ***PASSAGES, PREDICTABLE CRISES OF ADULT LIFE.*** The phenomena popularly know as "the mid-life crisis" usually begins in the late thirties or early forties. The question that seems to be uppermost in one's mind during this phase is "How much more time do I have left to live?" rather than how much time has elapsed since birth.

The notion of possibly becoming a "plateaued employee" occurred while Richard was attending a "Counseling the Plateaued Employee" seminar produced by the local university. The facilitator of the seminar outlined numerous Work Symptoms: an increase in the number of hours worked with no increase in output, due dates being missed, work needing to be redone, incomplete work, routine tasks taking longer, work being put off, doing only what is required, no apparent new ideas, etc. In other words, things just not getting done. As he absorbed the list, Richard realized he could put a check mark beside nearly all of the recognized symptoms.

Coupled with his overall passiveness and his "I don't care" attitude about work, was his growing feeling of noninvolvement. He was aware that he was withdrawing from people socially while he was having trouble working with them. This, of course, is the death knell for a human resource professional. He felt an overall lack of initiative and energy. He noticed in the last few months that he had no specific goals and no time frame.

Richard also used a passive form of aggression, which involved overt agreement but basic noncompliance. He would, for example, make a commitment to his boss to a due date for a project and then deliberately ignore the date. He found he was unable to make firm decisions. During this period minor problems became very upsetting. He felt fears he never had before. He mistrusted others, and had a strong feeling of urgency about time. For the first time in his life, Richard caught himself seeking reassurance that he was liked.

He was also becoming more forgetful. Living in the past, frequently referring to the so-called "good old days' was becoming part of his daily routine. He was losing his sense of what was really important to the business.

At times Richard found himself to be pushy or hostile. He had the feeling he was being excluded from the inside information which his peers were privy to. He had no long-range perspective anymore. He worked long hours, but was not productive or creative. There was a quality of "busy-ness" to his work. He constantly complained of being too busy at home and too busy at work to have any time for himself.

Richard also suffered an increase in colds and flu symptoms. He seemed to always be ill. He had become a self-centered hypochondriac. He became more and more isolated, which concerned his wife, Patricia, his sister, Roberta and his friends. His manager at work had noticed the change in his work habits and was also concerned.

Of all life's transitions, mid-life has been awarded top billing in recent years and not only by mental health professionals. Anyone who reads popular magazines or watches TV talk shows cannot avoid hearing about the mid-life crisis. Striking at no specific age (usually somewhere in the late thirties or early forties) it refers to those confusing, disturbing, conflicting emotions that are suffered whenever the message "You are no longer young," is picked up.

With the huge numbers of "Baby Boomers" moving into this age group, Richard noticed there was more information becoming available about the subject. He read that the mid-life crisis often involves giving up a particular dream, such as in the case of the scientist who realizes he will never win the Nobel Prize or the actor who will never take an Oscar home. Our dreams may be merely vague yearnings "to be someone," " to go somewhere," to be noticed, to excel, to be applauded.

Richard, like many others, found that with the mid-life crisis comes the reality that one's life dream will probably not come true. There's not going to be any pot of gold at the end of the rainbow. He found that along with accepting reality comes a tendency to look back, to pinpoint past mistakes. A man may agonize over a long list of I should have's: "I should have gone to college." "I should have taken that other job." "I should have invested in that stock or that piece of land."

In discussing this with his wife and sister they explained that the same thinking process happens with women. A woman may obsess about the man she did not marry, the career she sacrificed for her children, or the children she gave up for her career.

Richard discovered this was the time to find someone to blame (wife, husband, children, teacher, parents, bosses). Some people see it also as a time for change before it is too late and rush to try a new line of work, a new place to live, a new wife, husband, lover or companion.

Others may pass through the transition with little drama, willing to accept the message "you are no longer young" as an inescapable fact of life. Even so, there's no denying that almost everyone has moments of nostalgia, One of Richard's friends quoted Bishop Earnest Fitzgerald of Atlanta who wrote an article published in the Piedmont Airlines magazine entitled "Keep Chasing Those Dreams." The Bishop points to a newspaper study citing one of the perils of the crisis of the middle years as the loss of one's dreams. In our earlier years we have high and worthy ideals and ambitions, but as the years slip away we tend to lose sight of them. According to some psychologists, such a phenomenon happens to everyone. As we grow older, we lose our dreams. The article went on to state that there is a measure of truth in this contention. Many of us do lose our dreams with the passing years, but to say this process is inevitable requires more evidence than the circumstances present.

Richard discovered through netliving with older people that ***IT IS POSSIBLE TO BE A DREAMER TO THE VERY END.*** Dreams are essential to meaningful life. There is an old legend about a soldier who was court-marshaled before Alexander the Great. Dissatisfied with the verdict, the soldier asked for permission to appeal his case. Alexander quickly informed the soldier there was no higher court. The soldier replied, "Then I appeal my case from Alexander the SMALL to Alexander the GREAT."

There is an important lesson to be learned here -- all of us possess at least two selves. Both struggle for supremacy. The lower self, content to wander along the "Misty Flats" without purpose or direction, is willing to settle for things as they are. No new brave resolves are made, and there is no deep soul-searching for trouble. Many people succumb to this lower self. They settle down in the stagnant waters of unrealized potential. "I am too old to do this or that" or "I can't get that job because I'm too old."

Richard feared he was beginning to feel this way. But as he continued to read he began to experience a sense of hope. There is a another self all of us possess, unless it has been stifled or suppressed. It is the voice within us that tells us no matter what heights we have scaled, there are still more peaks to climb. The voice of that self will never let us rest on achieved victories, no matter how great they were . This voice tells us we are made for higher things.

Richard learned it was this voice that Mother Teresa listened to in Calcutta, India. It is the voice of the higher self that we need to hear. There are people who would tell us that dreaming of impossible aspirations and goals could result in unhealthy frustrations. This doesn't need to happen.

We may not achieve the goals or all of our dreams, Richard read, but even a partial victory brings a sense of well being and accomplishment. As students we always tried for the "A" grade, but if we gave it our best shot and received a "B," we felt pretty good about ourselves. It is the dreamer who brings about changes in our world and who finds the real satisfaction of living. Doctor Martin Luther King Junior is one of the best examples of a dreamer who made things happen.

Dreamers, Richard observed, have explored the earth and charted the heavens, they have been responsible for our greatest inventions. It is the dreamer who leaves the world a better place.

Richard discovered the middle and older years need not be years of lost dreams. Indeed, these years can be the most productive of all. A study of "THE BIOGRAPHIES OF GREAT PEOPLE" reveals that those who have made the greatest contributions have made them not while they were young, but when they were older.

He sighted some examples -- Florence Nightingale, who lived to be ninety, developed the first program for training nurses at Saint Thomas Hospital in London at the age of sixty-five. Otto Von Bismarck lived to be eighty-three and was active and alert until his death. He was the most capable and successful German statesman of modern times. Benjamin Franklin lived to be eighty-four years old, and at the age of eighty-one in 1787, was chosen a delegate to the convention that drew up the Constitution of the United States of America. Bob Hope and the late George Burns are entertainers who are good examples of older people who remained alert and active into their nineties.

Richard realized through netliving that you don't have to be a well known celebrity to be a dreamer. In his home town there is an older gentleman known as the "Golden Eagle." He is referred to as such because, as a retired human resource executive for a Fortune 500 company, he had dreamed for years of flying his own airplane and did so with gusto. With his family raised and full time employment behind him, he began by taking flying lessons. Within a year he received his private pilot's license. Then, only a few years later, on November 11, 1987, he returned safely home from a 25,000 mile solo flight to Australia and back at the ripe age of sixty-seven. Later Richard found himself on a committee with this gentleman and enjoyed listening to his great flying stories.

A Clevelander named Robert Manry also had a dream. Following a long career with the now defunct newspaper, the Cleveland Press, he dreamed of sailing his tiny boat the "Tinker

Bell" across the Atlantic. He began building the sailboat in his garage. At the age of sixty, Robert Manry crossed the Atlantic Ocean alone, in a fourteen foot sailboat.

Mr. Lou Holtz, the former successful Notre Dame head football coach, once said, "Deep down inside you'd better have a dream and you'd better have a goal or things don't happen." He said the only reason be became head coach at Notre Dame was because of his dreams and goals.

Richard concluded that the verdict of human experience is clear -- never stop dreaming. We may not live to achieve all of our dreams, but those who keep establishing goals and work toward them are likely to achieve far more than those without dreams.

THE OLDER YOU GET, THE BETTER YOU GET, LIKE FINE WINE. This may be a cliché, but often clichés are based on a verifiable truth. Richard had the opportunity to netlive with some active, outgoing older people attending Elder Hostels and discovered that there are many positive aspects to growing older.

A friend that Richard had worked with for many years has been retired for eight years and is a disciple of Dr. Walter M. Bortz II, who wrote "We Live Too Short and Die Too Long." He feels that "virtually everything we've previously thought about growing older has been wrong. All the recent information on aging is good news."

A combination of diet, exercise and attitude determines how well the 70-80 and even ninety-year-old person functions. Ninety-year-old muscles can be maintained and bones don't break if you use them. Arteries enlarge if you take care of them. Even the brain stays sharp if it's used. Excluding people with Alzheimer's disease, research shows that aging does not necessarily result in memory loss.

Richard's retired friend pointed out that the quality of aging is a self-fulfilling prophecy. If we have a negative attitude toward aging and expect the worst, the worst will come to pass. But age itself isn't what locks us into a limited lifestyle; it's how we age that's important.

Convinced the future holds many opportunities for people of all ages, Richard's friend pointed to some positive characteristics you gain as you grow older:

EXPERIENCE AND PERSPECTIVE. Younger people have a narrow perspective on life and can be overwhelmed when crises arise, even viewing them as insurmountable hurdles. But older people who have experienced hard times realize difficulties usually are temporary bumps in the road.

WISDOM. As you age, you have a greater capacity to see the whole picture rather than just part of it. The older person has been young before and knows what it's like, whereas the young person doesn't know what it's like to be older.

CONFIDENCE. The older you get, the less self-conscious you become. You make choices to please yourself, not others.

COPING. Your ability to manage stress improves with age. You are better able to cope with the adversities of life and you become more sure of yourself.

ATTITUDES ABOUT AGING. There's a younger attitude among older people these days. Today's 60-year-old is very different from a 60-year-old in the 1940s.

TIME TO ENJOY LIFE. Many younger people are in a big hurry because they feel that need to see so many things and to accomplish so much. An older person has already fulfilled many needs and feels free to enjoy life at a relaxed pace.

LESS ANXIETY ABOUT DEATH. Young people are afraid of dying because it's not yet time. They have youngsters depending on them. But as you age and live a long, full life, you can reduce that anxiety.

HAVE AN ESTABLISHED SAFETY NET. Successful older people have developed a habit of netliving with a safety network in place that they can utilize in times of sorrow as well as joy. They also reach out to the members in their network when there is a need.

Richard's retired friend adopted many of Dr. Bortz recommendations for longevity that will allow him to age successfully. Here is a list of the guidelines he has put into practice and according to Richard, he is living proof that they work:

* Exercise at least 30 minutes, four times a week.
* Choose an activity that is sustained, rhythmic, vigorous and enjoyable.
* Eat lots of fruits, whole grains, vegetables and lean poultry and fish.
* Get adequate rest and sleep.
* Keep your sense of humor and avoid anger. Try to maintain an optimistic outlook.
* Look for the good in everyone.
* Accept mental and physical challenges, and set goals that keep your life lively and creative.
* Take responsibility for your health and well-being. Don't rely on others to take care of you.
* Become involved in projects, programs and activities. Volunteer to help others. (Volunteers have better health and longer lifespans).
* Stay active. Don't use your age as an excuse to slow down or hide out at home.
* Develop a safety net of relatives and close friends to share your good and bad times and to netlive with on a regular basis. It must be a two-way street.

Richard joined a support group and is actively netliving with them to develop some new hobbies and interests to help him navigate a successful aging voyage.

NETLIVING NOTES:

* Netliving will help you understand the "Plateaued employee." I've learned the inner peace I achieve as I grow spiritually enables me to provide for all my needs.
* Netliving will induce you to make your dreams come true. I've learned that apart from nature, all that is good and beautiful in this world has come from human inventions and discoveries.

* Netliving will assist you in finding the good things about growing older. I've learned that if I eat a balanced diet, exercise daily and have a positive attitude and a strong spiritual life that my 70's and 80's will be okay.

CHAPTER ELEVEN

SECOND CAREERS

"Vitality shows in not only the ability to persist, but in the ability to start over."

F. Scott Fitzgerald
(1896-1940)

One of the characteristics of the nineties is early separation of employees from their organizations on an involuntary basis. Some of these partings occur as a result of restructuring, some because of leveraged buyout, some because of bankruptcy and some as the result of a clash with corporate leadership. Other early separations occur because of a merger with another, larger corporation. The politically correct term is "downsizing" or "rightsizing." The net result is that human beings, who have been active and productive all their working lives, are thrown out the door like yesterday's newspaper.

Roberta became aware of this trend in the late eighties and decided to "make lemonade out of the lemons that were being dished out." She began researching and netliving the field of outplacement, talking with colleagues who had used this type of service and some who had joined outplacement firms.

She found there were some national concerns who were full-service operations. They offered career transition assistance for all levels of the organization. Career decision consulting was offered to individuals. Restructuring consulting was offered to the key managers in a troubled firm.

Roberta found that these national concerns offered career management consulting and organizational consulting, as well as spouse employment assistance. In some cases, these firms had more than one hundred locations throughout the U.S. and Canada. There were some regional companies which were located in tri-state areas that had up to a dozen locations.

Roberta also found there were local concerns that had as many as three offices in one city.

Armed with this information, Roberta decided to target regional operations. She had searched her alumni directory to see if any of her college friends were employed by one of the target firms. She also consulted her human resource directory to make a list of those members who were in some way connected to the outplacement industry.

Roberta then began to netlive to find the next position in her career. She inquired about the principals of the company. Were they trustworthy individuals? Did they treat their associates with respect and fairness? Were they an ethical organization? How had their track record been for the past five years? What was the reason for the job opportunity being available?

It was a slow but rewarding process. Roberta had a chance to renew some old friendships and learn the "jargon" of the outplacement industry. She kept detailed notes on all the phone conversations she had and reviewed them on a weekly basis.

Finally, after a six-month search, Roberta received an offer from a regional outplacement company, one that she felt was the best in their field. In her interviews with the firm, she was told she would assist employers with restructuring issues within the organization.. She would be expected to help separated employees develop strategies to achieve their career objectives -- including re-employment, self-improvement, or retirement. She was also expected to help clients and their workforce to become more effective and productive in an increasingly competitive, global economy.

Before making her final decision, Roberta sat down for several hours with her brother, Richard and used him as a sounding board. She reviewed all the interviews she had had with this firm and the areas of concern she had. They poured over the firms literature to determine the strengths and weaknesses. They talked back and forth about the pluses and minuses of the position. They took a blank sheet of paper, as their father had taught them many years ago, and drew a straight line down the middle. At the top of the left side of the paper they headed "pros" and on the right they printed "cons."

After four hours of this intense analysis they came up with ten pro items and one con item on the right side of the paper. The only real concern that Roberta had was the amount of time she would be on the road traveling. Richard pointed out that most similar positions would require at least 30% travel and this one indicated only 25% would be required.

The portion of the position that most appealed to her compassionate nature was the valuable help she could give to the separated people. Roberta knew that, whatever the reasons and however prepared these individuals may have been for the loss of their jobs, they would experience a variety of emotions for the next few months. These feelings would range from fear and anger to shock, disappointment, confusion, and hopefully in some cases, sheer delight for the chance to move on to something new and exciting.

During the first week of her new assignment, Roberta learned the zoning-in process of the firm. First she was taught how to bolster the self-esteem of the outplaced person. She learned to stress that it is NOT what happens to you in life that matters, it is HOW YOU REACT to what happens that matters. Unexpected job loss or career change can be seen either as a crisis or as an opportunity. Many people focus only on the crisis and miss the opportunity to get what they really want in the next job or career.

Roberta was instructed that, basically, jobs are opportunities to solve problems. Since there is no shortage of problems in the world, there is no shortage of job opportunities. The secret is to be part of the SOLUTION, not part of the PROBLEM. She was taught to impress on the people that they are the center of their work life. The next job or career opportunity will be the result of the actions they take and the choices they make. They must be willing to work smarter, not harder, in their job or career search.

The approach Roberta was taught is basic: To get what you want, you must first know yourself, then what your target is and the direction to take. Without clear direction or purpose, you are likely to settle for whatever comes along.

Roberta was directed to instill a deeper purpose, to more closely align a person's work and personal life. She was to expand the client's ability to enter the work world in a way which produces satisfaction and vitality for them and value for others -- in short, a job that works for them. She was to stress that it is not easy to obtain what you want in a competitive job market. As in all human endeavors, there are difficulties. They will constantly face the question whether to stand up to the difficulties and take the next step or lay back and let the difficulties roll over them. She was encouraged to help make them winners in the job game.

The message Roberta was to relay to her clients was that it is not always the most qualified candidates who obtain the best positions, but those who are the most skilled at job search. This gives them a competitive edge. She was to remind them that when one door closes on a chapter of life, another one opens on a new and sometimes better chapter.

To better understand common mistakes that should be avoided by these job seekers, Roberta was given a list to emphasize the importance to avoid: not having a direction or focus; not knowing their own skills and abilities; not researching the job market; being overcome by desperation and discouragement; not getting proper support form home; having obsolete, outdated job skills; not knowing how to write an effective resume; improperly handling interview questions; not knowing what questions to ask; being ignorant about salary information; not using friends and relatives properly for netliving; and not devoting sufficient effort to search procedures.

At this point Roberta was ready and anxious to take on her first outplacement assignment. This assignment involved a grocery chain that was closing one of its local stores. Most of the employees found new positions in a relatively short period of time. The Produce Manager was another matter. He was in his late fifties and had been with the store for thirty years. He had a strong track record, making attractive displays to entice his customers to buy more. His main problem, as Roberta could see, was that he had passed that magic "fiftieth" birthday. An article in the Winter 1989 issue of HUMAN RESOURCE

MANAGEMENT pointed out that statistics show that from age forty until age fifty, the chance of obtaining employment drops ten percent each year.

After months of market research identifying options and netliving to build relationships, there were still no solid job offers. Roberta was concerned about the morale of her client and the fact that he might never find full-time employment. They talked about part-time work but he felt he needed to have a full-time job in order to qualify for important benefits.

After hours of brain-storming, assessing his likes and dislikes, an idea finally surfaced--the produce manager would like to repair and rebuild bicycles. From a young age he had been naturally skilled at repairing bicycles. He had always been the guy sought out by neighborhood children when their "wheels" were broken. He enjoyed seeing the smiles on their faces when the job was done.

Using his netliving skills, Roberta's client made contacts with the rubbish removal drivers in the surrounding communities. He indicated that he would pay them a few dollars for every usable bike frame, wheel or part they delivered from their weekly rounds. This was the raw material for his new business. He set up shop in his garage and, within a relatively short period of time, his new career was thriving and he was happier than he had been in the past year.

His community had a Council of Small Enterprises that was part of the local Chamber of Commerce and through netliving with some of the local members he was able to purchase medical insurance for his wife and himself at a reasonable cost. In addition he was pleasantly surprised by his tax accountant to find that a portion of that cost was tax deductible.

Roberta's next client was to eventually become known as the "silver eagle." He had spent thirty-five years with a fortune 500 company as a human resource executive. His most recent position had been vice president of human resources for the entire corporation. With the passing of time and the introduction of new technology, the workplace environment didn't feel as comfortable for him as it had in the past, so he began putting out feelers regarding a possible early retirement buy-out.

He had been involved in hundreds of such arrangements, but from the other side of the desk. He admitted to Roberta that it was a strange, almost "out-of-body" experience, going through this transition. The reason Roberta had became involved was that the executive's firm had a contract with Roberta's organization. The outplacement package was a "sweetener" to his overall retirement buy-out package.

Roberta felt a bit like the student trying to tutor the teacher. This individual client had conducted much more career counseling than she had. However, he quickly indicated that the situation was much different since he was personally involved.

They began the process of self-understanding by assessing the likes and dislikes encountered during his working years. While employed he had performed a significant amount of volunteer work at his alma mater and had served on a committee to help displaced workers find new careers. Although he enjoyed these activities, he wanted to try something completely different in this new chapter of his life. His previous activities seemed too earth-bound.

Through much probing and discussion, Roberta discovered her client had always wanted to fly an aircraft. They looked into flying lessons at a local airport and the rest is history. The client took to flying like he had been doing it all his life. He progressed rapidly and soloed in record time. When he received his pilot's license, one of his first passengers, after his immediate family, was Roberta.

The thought of her first ride in a Cessna 182 Skylane made her a bit nervous, but a few minutes after they were airborne, she began to relax as she enjoyed the panoramic view of the familiar countryside. Taking the controls for a short period of time added to the thrill of Roberta's first flight in a small aircraft.

During this period of learning how to fly, her client had just rented available aircraft. However, he had been saving for many years to own his own plane and as soon as he knew he had passed the final test he placed an order for his own Cessna. Netliving played an important part in deciding what optional items he would require on the new purchase.

The pilot's first long solo flight took him from Ohio to California. When he completed that flight successfully, he began making plans to follow the same flight plan as Charles Lindbergh many years before. This dream required the installation of some special equipment and additional fuel tanks necessary for the transatlantic flight. After much planning and practice, he launched his adventurous flight across the "big pond."

Roberta could not believe how much younger he looked after being involved with flying for a year or so. One day, while having lunch with her at the airport, he confided that he was planning to make an around-the-world solo flight within the next six months. He admitted his wife was not too pleased with the prospect, but she had grudgingly given her blessing.

After months of planning and testing equipment, he took off from Ohio and headed west, making stops all around the world. The pilot was greeted at every landing by crowds of well-wishers and he had a huge reception when he finally arrived on his home field a week later. Roberta joined the crowd waiting to greet him as he taxied up to the terminal. It was a joy to see the satisfied look on his face.

Ironically, the Silver Eagle crashed his plane on a short, routine test flight from his home base. Fortunately, he was not seriously injured and within a few months was back in the sky.

When Roberta first planned a client's job-seeking campaign, she learned that many key executives yearn to own or operate their own business. Such ventures are unlikely to be typical retail franchise operations. They are more likely to involve launching or acquiring a consulting activity or perhaps building a company around a new product or service.

Roberta's new clients were a husband and wife who had worked in different departments at the same firm for twenty-five years. They dreamed of owning a bed and breakfast somewhere on an ocean beach along the east coast of the United States. They had been netliving with current owners of bed and breakfast establishments and had been planning the venture for about five years before their employer announced a reorganization plan and the subsequent early retirement buy-out.

The adventurous couple jumped at the opportunity. They would not only receive enhanced retirement benefits but would also be given a buy-out bonus and the services of Roberta's organization.

In addition to their spade work, Roberta was able to add to their netliving and suggested several targeted areas to help make their dream a reality. They took some vacation time and drove down the Carolina coast to visit three locations. Starting in South Carolina, they slowly worked their way north. The first two properties they visited did not fit their specifications.

The third property, in North Carolina, did meet the criteria. They fell in love with it immediately. The building was in need of some minor repairs, but they were excited to find that, if they purchased this particular piece of ocean front real estate, they would be the only bed and breakfast for fifteen miles in either direction. The only barrier between their dream bed and breakfast and the ocean was sand dunes.

Their report to Roberta was filled with elation and joy. The husband had been happily raised by his grandparents on a similar beach in New Jersey. To him this old inn was truly special. They invited Roberta to look the place over the week they took possession. Painters, roofers, plumbers and their grown children worked on various aspects of the building. The two ground floor suites were transformed. Their living quarters and the rest of the rambling inn were made comfortable and inviting. On any given night they were capable of providing sleeping arrangement for two dozen adults. There were provisions where several children could sleep in each of the suites.

As they were busy working to get their new business off the ground, a young couple stopped by to see if they could make a reservation for Easter weekend, only two weeks away. The husband informed them that the bed and breakfast was not officially open for business but invited them to look around. The wife offered them a cup of coffee and as they talked she learned that the young couple was in the military. They would soon be separated by military assignment and therefore wanted some time to walk the beach together.

The new owners relented and the young military couple became their first official guests during the Easter weekend. Four years later, what they thought would only be a seasonal business had turned into a full-time, year-round activity.

They had always been effective netlivers and were able to develop a strong network in this new community. Their oldest son came to visit while they were in the "fixing up" phase and he also fell in love with the area. He liked it so well he convinced his former college roommate to go into business with him. They bought a bar on the beach near his parent's business location.

Their newly married son had the same experience. He liked the area so well that he netlived within his current organization and arranged a transfer to a nearby town. The only member of their immediate family still remaining in New Jersey was their soon-to-be- married daughter.

Roberta felt a true sense of accomplishment by being part of this couple's dream come true.

Very few positions, if any, at the key executive level are successfully filled through the "Help Wanted" section of local, or even national, publications. A study conducted by the Bureau of National Affairs during the late eighties discovered that seventy percent of key positions are filled by netliving. One gets to be a finalist for these positions by effectively building a network of personal and professional contacts who provide the candidate with helpful introductions and leads. This is true for current and potential openings, and most certainly true for positions that are "created" to meet unique needs with special talent.

Roberta had just such a unique situation. Her client came from a prominent financial services institution. The client's compensation was $165,000, plus a bonus and a leased automobile. She had been with the organization for ten years and had enjoyed great success with one promotion after another. Nine months prior to her meeting Roberta, her organization chart reporting relationship had changed in a major way. As often happens, significant problems developed in the new relationship and she ultimately found herself in an outplacement situation.

When she arrived for her first meeting with Roberta, she was very embittered by the termination and totally disenchanted with the banking profession in general. She was adamant about having no further affiliation with the banking industry. Again, not an unusual reaction after such a painful experience.

Roberta began the process by thoroughly debriefing the client regarding her background and work experience. Interestingly, for several years, between completing her undergraduate work at Yale and commencing New York University's M.B.A. program, she had worked in the Peace Corps. She said that these were three of the most satisfying years of her life. Since income amount was not the prime concern and because she was interested in the Third World and enjoyed making a contribution to the welfare of others, she decided to explore non-banking related opportunities.

Roberta and her client began an extensive examination of a wide range of job opportunities: governmental, quasi-governmental, non-profit foundations, etc., as well as business other than banking which could capitalize on her financial services background. After completing the assessment and planning phase of her job hunting program, she embarked on an active netliving campaign. She carefully explored selected areas of interest and found a reasonable degree of receptivity in each.

But the more Roberta worked with her candidate and the better she got to know her, the clearer it became to both of them that she was a superb banker. She owed it to herself to explore appropriate opportunities in the familiar banking environment as well as other, more novel areas. If she did not explore further, Roberta felt she would do herself a disservice and the banking industry would have lost a real asset. At first, the client was predictably resistant to the thought of putting "bankers" on her netliving list. She was finally persuaded when Roberta pointed out that it was the bankers who could be expected to open doors to a wide variety of organizations on her target list, including the large foundations.

A month or so later, during a netliving meeting with a banking officer, she heard that individual say, "It's interesting you've come to see me today. We've been thinking of expanding our presence in the Pacific Rim. If we were to do so, would you be interested in such a spot?" Little by little the pieces of the job fell into place and she was presented with an offer she accepted. It was a position in which she could not fail since it had literally been built around her. The most successful on-the-job accomplishments are by people who truly fit their jobs.

While working at the outplacement position, Roberta had one dismal failure. Her client was a chemist who had worked for a manufacturing company. This woman had worked for the firm for twenty years and it was bought out by a German company. It seemed that the foreign company had another similar facility less than one hundred miles away and immediately decided to merge Roberta's client's lab with their existing lab in the other city.

For some strange reason this client took an instant dislike to Roberta and no matter what suggestions she made this client found fault with them. Roberta netlived with her fellow outplacement specialists to obtain some advice on how to handle this character.

After several more weeks of trying different approaches, Roberta was ready to throw in the towel. She spoke with her immediate supervisor and asked for some suggestions. After a long discussion they jointly decided to turn the assignment over to a male counterpart. That did the trick for the client, but it was a hard pill for Roberta to swallow.

Regardless, Roberta spent many successful years with this regional out-placement firm. During her tenure she not only was paid well but she received much satisfaction from seeing people placed in positions that were a good fit for them and made them happy at their work.

NETLIVING NOTES:

* Netliving will improve your second career search. I've learned that offering help to someone who asks makes me more comfortable in asking for help when I need it.
* Netliving will enhance your new business development. I've learned that "Word-of-mouth" is the best form of advertising.
* Netliving will help create new, unique positions for you. I've learned that being open to new ideas and people creates opportunities.

CHAPTER TWELVE

TO VOLUNTEERISM AND GOOD HEALTH

"That larger vision is certain to make clear the value in our own lives of service to others."
Lucy Larcom (1824-1893)

Early in his human resource career Richard became involved in volunteerism. His first experience was as the chairman of his employer's United Way campaign. This role taught him the importance of surrounding himself with a good team of workers. Like everything else Richard undertook, he went after attaining the United Way goal with a vengeance (the goal had been set for him by his manager and the president of the company).

His team was enthusiastic about this worthwhile cause, which made his job as chairman much easier. Representatives from each department attended the kickoff meeting. Before proceeding, the first order of business was to make sure all the volunteers from each department had signed a pledge card. He had learned in the chairman's training class to get his team signed up first. It is difficult for a solicitor to feel a deep conviction for a program unless he /she has contributed to it, he thought.

Richard opened the meeting by giving a "rah-rah" speech on volunteerism: He titled it VOLUNTEERISM -- THE TRIPLE PLAY OF THE BUSINESS WORLD.

He began by saying, "Although the baseball season has passed I would like to use the analogy of a 'triple play' to compare the benefits companies with volunteer programs receive.

"A triple play in baseball is made up of three outs in one single play. In baseball we may experience only one or two triple plays a season, in all of major league baseball. They are rare and desirable because the team that makes the triple play stands a much better chance of winning. In the business world, as in baseball, the name of the game is winning.

"Volunteerism is a win--win--win situation. In business you can have a triple play every day. When an organization has an effective volunteer program, all involved benefit. First, the employer wins. Second, the employee wins. And, third and most importantly, the community wins.

"First the employer wins -- employers who offer volunteer programs help employees reach out to their communities and reap benefits above and beyond just a clear conscience.

"Volunteer work improves morale and enhances the image of the employer in the eyes of the community. In the case of a consumer-oriented company which makes and sells a product purchased by the community, it is a double barreled benefit.

"Other benefits for the company according to surveyed executives show some specific skills are significantly enhanced by volunteer participation including the following:

* Communication skills - written and verbal
* Organizational and time management skills
* 'People' skills -- caring, listening, & negotiating
* Accountability and assessment reporting
* Planning skills, short and long-term objectives
* Budgeting and allocation skills
* Survival skills - stress management, personal priorities."

Richard pointed out that often more important than building specific skills is fostering changed attitudes about work and society. The following attitudes observed in volunteer participants shape the workplace and its outcomes:

* Increased understanding of co-workers and respect for diversity
* More innovative approaches in response to difficulties
* Enhancement of calculated risk taking
* Heightened appreciation for benefits provided by employers
* Enlarged sense of community and social obligation

* Greater appreciation for contributions from all levels of the organization.
* Affirmation of personal capability and worth
* Development of habits of pride and responsibility
* Positive resistance to feelings of isolation and alienation

Secondly, the employee wins -- Volunteering not only improves employee skills and attitudes, but also provides opportunities for growth through positive contacts with other business, government agencies, and with potential clients and markets.

A highly selective sample of executives surveyed for the National College Graduate Survey on Volunteering listed, among others, the following professional benefits gained through volunteering:

* New business contacts
* Experience in strategic planning
* Experience in working with different constituencies
* Better understanding of government policies and regulations
* Opportunity to work with leaders and others in the community

One-third of the executives interviewed mentioned the role of community service in professional advancement. For some, an evaluation of volunteer activities is part of the periodic performance review.

Physical and psychological benefits -- Several studies conducted at Michigan State University have examined the relationship between altruistic or helping behaviors and health or hardiness. The number of professional journal articles dealing with this subject has tripled in the last five years. These studies are not explicitly concerned with such behaviors in the corporate environment, but their conclusions extend to the workplace and suggest a further rationale for volunteer programs.

The connection of helping behaviors to stress reduction, self esteem, socialization and optimistic outlook implies a connection to overall health. Anecdotal evidence of the health benefits of helping behaviors abound. In a survey of more than 3,000 volunteers conducted by the American Association of Retired Persons (AARP), over 90% reported that regular volunteering had produced feelings that alleviated stress-related physical symptoms. This same survey attributes strengthened immunity and relief from certain chronic conditions to active helping behaviors.

Richard noted that among the seventy-five retirees who came to the company's recent Thanksgiving dinner, a number looked extraordinarily healthy and vigorous. In talking to those who looked younger and more relaxed, he notice they were quick to tell how much they were helping and volunteering in their neighborhoods.

Thirdly, the community wins -- Survey respondents, Richard pointed out, targeted the following issues in their designated volunteer projects:

1) Education
2) Health
3) Youth in Crisis
4) Environment
5) Homelessness

He went on to point out that volunteer centers in U.S. cities nationwide affirm the local benefit from corporate volunteer activities in the schools. Volunteer centers, which act as referral agents to nonprofit organizations, report that one of the most consistently brokered services is elementary and secondary school assistance. The success of these programs builds increasing demand.

For example, Tenneco Inc. began its partnership with Jefferson Davis High School in Houston, Texas in 1981. The school was targeted for special attention because test scores there trailed others in the same school district. Emily Cole, principal at Jefferson Davis, points to some differences Tenneco had made in four years:

*Dropout/at-risk rates have fallen from 65% to 47%
*College acceptances have risen from 10% to 60%
*Average SAT scores have increased by approximately 100 points

Cole reported her school and the community have made gains beyond what they imagined possible when the partnership began.

Richard related that his company had also been involved with a local middle school for several years and all the feedback had been positive. The report on the attendance records of the student body improved. The drop-out rate and the test scores also showed improvement. He mentioned that new programs were introduced and were being nurtured by the volunteers.

An example of a new program was the junior Toastmasters program that he and a few of his fellow Toastmasters had introduced at the middle school. This scaled-down version was comprised of brief speeches and meetings geared to a shorter time frame. The students who participated really put their hears and souls into the program.

Richard concluded his speech by pointing out that there were many different volunteer programs functioning in the area. He mentioned that their company had joined the Business Volunteerism Council and had surveyed their employees for volunteering ideas. He mentioned that an advisory committee was being formed and all segments of the business were encouraged to become involved.

Once the committee was formed and organized, various community agencies were invited to talk to employees about the help that was needed. Representatives from the Food Bank and the Harvest for Hunger spoke, in addition to members of the Adopt-a-School program.

The United Way campaign had been successful in the past and Richard aimed to make it successful again. With that, he concluded the meeting by emphasizing that volunteerism is a triple play -- win-win-win.

In reflecting on his personal experience as a volunteer, Richard recalled some happy times. He had always been fond of babies, and when he was approached to be a volunteer for the March of Dimes Walk America program, he jumped in with both feet. There would be an organized twenty-five mile walk through the city streets with refreshment stands at intervals along the way.

As captain of his team Richard had to find people who would not only walk the twenty-five mile course, but would be willing to approach their relatives and friends to sponsor them at a generous amount per mile for the full number of miles walked.

At first the thought of finding willing volunteers was more difficult than the actual walking. Later, with experience, it became easier for Richard to approach people and point out the great benefits the March of Dimes accomplished through study and research. Richard was grateful that his own three children were born healthy; this fact served to increase his enthusiasm for helping those less fortunate.

Eventually Richard was brought into another program designed to serve the needs of children suffering from fatal diseases. Make-a-Wish is a program that helps dying children enjoy their final days on this earth. Richard participated in many activities for this worthwhile cause. These activities extended from participating on a volleyball team to raise money to selling hamburgers to the fans who had come out to watch the games. In his younger days, he participated in the annual Heart Run for the local chapter of the National Heart Association. Although he wasn't much of a speed runner, by putting one foot in front of the other he was able to run five and ten kilometer races for this worthy endeavor. He signed up sponsors who made substantial contributions for each completed kilometer.

Besides helping a worthwhile cause, Richard also developed himself physically by training for these races and gained the cardiovascular well-being that results from such demanding workouts. Another benefit Richard derived was the opportunity to meet many nice people who were involved. Most of them were caring individuals, interested in helping their fellow runners and supporting worthy endeavors. This was a demanding time in Richard's life but a fun period as well.

When Richard's brother-in-law contracted cancer, he and the whole family were emotionally devastated. One of the things Richard could do to help the situation was to participate in the American Cancer Society's annual bike-a-thon. This fund raiser was similar to the Heart Association's road race and the March of Dimes Walk America. It required him to sign up sponsors who would contribute for each mile completed of the twenty-five mile bike ride.

Richard and his long time bike riding friend became involved in this program and participated annually for many years during which they were able to collect many hundreds of dollars that went for cancer research. Richard witnessed firsthand the benefits his brother-in-law received from the American Cancer Society and felt his efforts were rewarded.

One of the things Richard looked forward to in his retirement years was having more available hours to netlive and volunteer with some great organizations. He had already been in touch with the R.S.V.P. group made up of retired volunteers. The initials stand for Retired Senior Volunteer Program. This group does many wonderful things such as reading local newspapers over the radio for blind listeners and recording books onto audio tapes. He found there are many worthwhile activities that this wonderful organization sponsors. One of his retired friends belongs to a little theater group which performs at homes for the elderly shut-ins. Another of his retired friends belongs to a singing group which visits nursing homes and veteran's hospitals to sing old favorites to entertain the patients.

These wonderful volunteer organizations make a significant difference in the quality of life for many of the citizens of our communities. The bonus for those who volunteer is they live happier and longer lives.

NETLIVING NOTES:

* Netliving will help you to expand your volunteering efforts. I've learned that feeling good about serving others less fortunate is the most basic requirement for my happiness.
* Netliving enhances your understanding of the benefits of volunteering. I've learned there have been scientific studies made confirming that those who volunteer live happier, healthier and longer lives.
* Netliving with other retirees will improve your quality of life. I've learned that becoming involved in the fabric of life by contacting many people on a regular basis keeps me sharp physically, mentally, emotionally and spiritually.

CHAPTER THIRTEEN

THE TWELVE-STEP PROGRAMS

"It is in our faults and failings, not in our virtues, that we touch one another and find sympathy."

Jerome K. Jerome

From the time of birth until the age of two, Roberta had been the dominant of the twins. She was the first born by a few minutes and was the leader for that time period. When the twins reached the age of the "terrible twos," Richard became more aggressive and she became shy and reserved. She was very much a "momma's girl." She would hide behind her mother's apron when a stranger came to the door. She was emotionally attached to her mother to the extent that going off to kindergarten for a few hours was a traumatic event. Finally, after much coaxing and cajoling, Roberta settled into a school-day routine. This methodical procedure went smoothly until the middle of the fourth grade.

One bright fall afternoon, Roberta came home from school and was startled to see a big blue ambulance parked at the front door of their modest bungalow. She burst through the front door. Her heart pounded as she saw her mother laying on the couch while EMS attendants worker over her. Roberta's father was there, along with her brother Richard and her aunt and uncle who lived nearby.

Numb with the initial shock of seeing her usually in-charge mother lying there so helpless, Roberta managed to ask what had happened. The sad story unfolded. Two of Roberta's cousins had come to visit their Aunt Mary to show her their new puppy. Roberta's mother was on a step ladder cleaning the living room ceiling when the puppy nipped one of the cousins. Roberta's poor mother "flew" off the ladder and landed on the floor with a loud thump.

Later Roberta learned that her mother's hip had been broken in four places. This was a serious trauma and recovery would require her to be hospitalized for several months. This was especially tough on Roberta since she could not remember ever being separated from her mother for any length of time -- in fact, they had never been separated, period. The hospital's policy did not allow young children to visit patients.

The best contact Roberta could manage was to stand outside the hospital and gaze up at the window of the room in which her mother was confined in traction slings. During this depressing time the only comfort Roberta found came form eating chocolate chip cookies by the box full. Her father tried to console her and her brother tried to help fill the emotional gap, all to no avail.

Roberta had been an excellent student in elementary school; now the quality of her study took a nose dive. She missed school often during her mother's hospital confinement. Her father was working "double duty" at the family dry cleaning business. He could not maintain close supervision on the two children, thus the decline in the quality of their home life and performance in school continued to mount.

When the inevitable report card came home, Roberta's father insisted she move in with her aunt and uncle for the remainder of her mother's hospitalization period. Roberta, chubby and self-conscious, resisted the idea of sharing a home with her four male cousins. To be living with these awful boys who constantly teased her was more than she could imagine she could survive.

After too long a time, Roberta's mother came home from the hospital and continued to recover with months of additional physical therapy. Roberta was pleased to have her cherished mother home again. But during her mother's absence, Roberta had formed some bad habits. These ranged from eating all the wrong things in large quantities to skipping her homework assignments. The result was she was in big trouble.

With the passage of time Roberta's life seemed to improve, then she contracted scarlet fever and was quarantined to the house for a month. Her school attendance did not meet the requirements and the school officials were forced to flunk her. She was devastated. She felt not only fat but stupid too. The other children made life miserable for her. She came home from school and threw herself on the couch, crying incessantly.

While in this valley of despair, a major change came over Roberta. She made up her mind she would never again be a failure. For her remaining school years and subsequently the rest of her life, she was always at the head of the class or the head of any organization with which she became affiliated. She was always a force with whom one had to reckon within that organization.

No matter what honors she received or how successful she subsequently became, Roberta always sensed there was something missing from her life. She felt a void within herself that somehow she could not fill with success and "power." The closest she came to feeling fulfilled was when she stuffed herself with food in quantities far beyond normal requirements. Food became her only true source of comfort, and the effects of this showed in a really big way.

Over the years Roberta gained more and more extra weight. Her five foot four inch frame was now carrying over two hundred pounds. Life had become difficult in all ways. Physically, she had difficulty moving around. Emotionally, she was angry all the time. In fact, the only emotion she could express was that of anger.

Spiritually she was in a bad way also. Although Roberta had been raised in a religious atmosphere, she was never really spiritual. She went through the motions and rituals out of respect for parental guidance but did not have a personal relationship with God.

One day while reading the daily newspaper she noticed something in Ann Landers' column and read about an organization called "Overeaters Anonymous." According to the article, this group follows a twelve-step program based on the twelve steps toward recovery utilized by "Alcoholics Anonymous." She reread the article and realized that many of the issues that were raised were the very issues with which Roberta was confronted. She phoned the local office of OA and had them send her a meeting list and some descriptive literature.

Roberta was usually not a procrastinator, but she was unsure about attending an OA meeting. After a few months of thinking about it, she finally reached down inside herself and came up with the nerve to attend her first OA meeting. When she arrived at the meeting room there were already about a dozen people sitting around chatting. The OA's were friendly and greeted her openly; this eased the level of Roberta's self-consciousness.

At 8:00 p.m. sharp the meeting began with the Serenity Prayer: "God grant me the serenity to accept the things I cannot change, the courage to change the things I can, and the wisdom to know the difference." As Roberta reflected on these strengthening words they made more and more sense to her. That little prayer is a navigation chart for anyone's life journey, she thought.

Next, the voluntary leader introduced herself by her first name and added that she was a compulsive overeater. She asked that each member do the same. They went around the room with each person present giving his or her first name and stating they were a compulsive overeater. When it was Roberta's turn she spoke the required words with difficulty. However, as she listened to what each person had to say, it became apparent that she shared a common problem with a large number of other individuals. She felt more and more at home with the other OA's as the meeting progressed. She noted that some of the members used words like anorexic and bulimic, that until now she did not know were connected with compulsive overeating. Some members also referred to themselves as "food addicts."

The leader next asked if there were any newcomers. Roberta raised her hand. The entire group applauded and gave her another feeling of warm welcome. They also handed her a newcomers' package which contained some of the basic information about Overeaters Anonymous and the twelve steps and twelve traditions of the organization.

Next on the agenda a member of the group read chapter five, "How it Works," from what is affectionately called "the big book" of Alcoholics Anonymous. "Rarely have we seen a person fail who has thoroughly followed our path . . . Our stories disclose, in a general way, what we used to be like, what happened, and what we are like now. . . Here are the steps we took, which are suggested as a program of recovery:

"1. We admitted we were powerless over food – that our lives had become unmanageable.
2. Came to believe that a Power greater than ourselves could restore us to sanity.
3. Made a decision to turn our will and our lives over to the care of God as we understood Him.
4. Made a searching and fearless moral inventory of ourselves.
5. Admitted to God, to ourselves and to another human being the exact nature of our wrongs.
6. Were entirely ready to have God remove all these defects of character.
7. Humbly asked Him to remove our shortcomings.
8. Made a list of all persons we had harmed, and became willing to make amends to them all.
9. Made direct amends to such people wherever possible, except when to do so would injure them or others.
10. Continued to take personal inventory and when we were wrong, promptly admitted it.
11. Sought through prayer and meditation to improve our conscious contact with God as we understood Him, praying only for knowledge of His will for us and the power to carry it out.
12. Having had a spiritual awakening as the result of these steps, we tried to carry this message to compulsive overeaters and to practice these principles in all our affairs."

Roberta felt overwhelmed when she heard all this. One of her first questions to the leader of the meeting was, "Do you have to belong to a certain religious denomination to be successful in OA?" Her quick response was no that there were members from all types of religious backgrounds. Even some atheists and agnostics belong to the group. They choose the group in most cases as their Higher Power in the beginning and that usually changes with the passage of time. The person sitting next to her told her not to be concerned and to "keep coming back." The new comrade explained that no one had been able to maintain anything like perfect compliance to these steps and principles. The point is that the principles are guides to progress. The program claims spiritual progress rather than spiritual perfection.

The leader went on to say that OA is a fellowship of men and women who meet to share their experience, strength and hope with one another in order that they may solve their common problem and help those who still suffer to recover from compulsive overeating. This, in Roberta's reasoning, was a solid example of netliving.

The leader went on clearly stating the purpose and methods of OA: "...To stop eating compulsively and we welcome in fellowship and friendly understanding all those who share our common problem. The common problem, we consider, is a three-fold disease; physical, emotional and spiritual. This disease has many different manifestations. Compulsive overeating leading to full blown food addiction is one aspect, but there is also anorexia and bulimia." On a recent Oprah show, one professional estimated that one million young men and boys suffer from eating disorders. A recent article in a scientific magazine estimated 300,000 people die annually from obesity and its complications. Like alcoholism and drug addiction, this disease is a killer that doesn't take' prisoners.

"Food addition/compulsive overeating is rampant in our society," the leader continued. "We consider it a more socially acceptable addiction, one with less stigma attached. We don't put people in jail for this disease. However, obese people are frequent targets for stereotypes and are labeled weak-willed, lazy and sometimes portrayed as evil. They are frequently the subjects of harsh jokes that tear down and destroy their self-esteem. The pain of this disease is real," she concluded.

Roberta could relate to everything she heard, especially the cruel jokes that people had aimed at her all her life. This had been devastating when she was a youngster. Other kids can be the most cruel of all attackers.

A volunteer stood up and recited a list of the "tools of recovery":

"ABSTINENCE - In OA, abstinence is the action of refraining from eating compulsively. There are no absolutes for abstinence. For some, abstinence facilitates working the twelve steps; for others, it comes from working the twelve steps. As a result of living the OA program of recovery, the symptom of compulsive eating is removed on a daily basis. Ultimately, we are abstinent because we no longer have the desire to eat compulsively. For many newcomers to get started, the old three-zero-one formula works. The abbreviation stands for three moderate meals a day with nothing in-between, doing it one day at a time."

For Roberta this was a new concept since she had always thought, based on religious teaching, that to "fast and abstain" meant the complete absence of a food substance such as meat or drink.

"SPONSORSHIP - Sponsors are OA members who are living the twelve steps and twelve traditions to the best of their ability. They are willing to share their recovery with other members of the Fellowship and are committed to abstinence. A sponsor is asked to help us through our program of recovery on all three levels: physical, emotional and spiritual. By netliving with other members of OA and sharing their experience, strength and hope, sponsors continually renew and reaffirm their own recovery. Sponsors share their program to the level of their own experience."

The leader pointed out that OA is a program of attraction: find a sponsor who has what you want and ask that person how he or she is achieving it. A member may work with more than one sponsor and may change sponsors at will.

"MEETINGS - Meetings are gatherings of two or more compulsive overeaters who come together to share their personal experience and the strength and hope OA has given them," the leader said "Though there are many types of meetings, netliving with other compulsive overeaters is the basis of them all. Meetings give us an opportunity to identify and confirm our common problem and share the gifts we receive through this program.

"TELEPHONE - The telephone is a way by which we can share, on a one-to-one basis, a way to avoid the isolation which is so common among us. Many members call other OA members and their own sponsors daily. As a part of the surrender process, it is a tool by which we learn to reach out, ask for help, and extend help to others. The telephone also provides an immediate outlet for those hard-to-handle situations we may experience.

"WRITING - In addition to writing our inventories and the list of people we have harmed, most members have found that writing has been an indispensable tool for working the steps. Further, putting our thoughts and feelings down on paper or describing a troubling incident helps us to better understand our actions and reactions in a way that is often not revealed to us by simply thinking or talking about them. In the past, compulsive eating was our most common reaction to life. When we put our difficulties down on paper, it becomes easier to see situations more clearly and perhaps better discern any necessary action.

"LITERATURE - OA members study and read OA literature including pamphlets, the books -- *Overeaters Anonymous* and *For Today* -- and *Lifeline,* our monthly journal of recovery. We also study the book, *Alcoholics Anonymous*, referred to as the Big Book, and the *Twelve Steps and Twelve Traditions*, another A.A. book, to understand and reinforce our program. Many OA's find that when they read on a daily basis, the literature further reinforces how to live the twelve steps. Our OA literature and the AA books are an ever-available tool that gives insight into our problem of eating compulsively, strength to deal with it, and the very real hope that there is a solution for us.

"ANONYMITY - Anonymity, referred to in traditions eleven and twelve, is a tool that guarantees that we will place principles before personalities. The protection anonymity provides offers each of us freedom of expression and safeguards us from gossip. Anonymity assures us that only we, as individual OA members, have the right to make our membership known within our community. Anonymity at the level of press, radio, films and television means that we never allow our last names or faces to be used once we identify ourselves as OA members. This protects both the individual and the Fellowship.

"Within the Fellowship, anonymity means that whatever we share with another OA member will be held in respect and confidence. What we hear at meetings should remain there. It should be understood, however, that anonymity must not be used to limit our effectiveness within the Fellowship. It is not a break of anonymity to use our full names within our group or OA service bodies. Also, it is not a break of anonymity to enlist twelfth-step help for group members in trouble, provided we are careful to refrain from discussing any specific personal information."

"Another aspect of anonymity is that we are all equal in the Fellowship, whether newcomer or seasoned old-timer; and our outside status makes no difference in OA. Also, we have no stars or VIP's. We come together simply as compulsive overeaters."

"SERVICE - Carrying the message to the compulsive overeater who still suffers is the basic purpose of our Fellowship and therefore the most fundamental form of service. Any service, no matter how small, that will help reach a fellow sufferer adds to the quality of our own recovery. Getting to meetings, putting away chairs, putting out literature, talking to newcomers, doing whatever needs to be done in a group or for OA as a whole are ways in which we give back what we have so generously been given. We are encouraged to do what we can when we can. ' A life of sane and happy usefulness' is what we are promised as the result of working the twelve steps. Service helps to fulfill that promise. As OA's responsibility Pledge states: 'Always to extend the hand and heart of OA to all who share my compulsion; for this, I am responsible.'"

At this point Roberta was so full of information she felt she was ready to burst. She asked herself, How will I ever be able to remember all of this good information? A female member sitting near her noticed her puzzled expression and told her there are many sayings in Overeaters Anonymous, and one of them is

"Easy does it." She felt that was appropriate in Roberta's current situation.

Roberta had been a netliver all her life but she never thought that her netliving skills could help her with her eating problem. She was finding out that OA was willing to accept her as she was now, as she had been and as she would be in the future. The members were understanding of the problems she faced now and were willing to share with others in the group. She found it easy to communicate with the other OA members as a result of their mutual understanding and acceptance. She also found a certain amount of relief, having found acceptance and understanding. The ability to communicate with others who had walked in her shoes and had found relief from their illness helped her toward self-acceptance and self-understanding.

The other revelation Roberta experienced at that first meeting was that by the acceptance and understanding of oneself, and by the support and companionship of the group, a new power and new way of life had been opened to her.

As she studied the literature and attended at least two OA meetings a week, Roberta became familiar with the program. She became abstinent the first week she was in the program and ate only three moderate meals a day with nothing in-between. After six months of being abstinent, attending meetings and following the steps, Roberta had lost thirty pounds. She was pleased with her progress with the weight loss, but more importantly she was learning a complete new way of living.

She had become more honest with herself and with others. Before entering the OA program she had been dishonest with everyone (especially herself) about little things as well as the significant matters. Roberta became more open to suggestions by other people. Her chosen sponsor was a mature lady who had been in the program fifteen years and had lost over one hundred pounds and maintained the loss over time. Roberta spoke with her sponsor every day for at least a few minutes. Roberta asked questions and the sponsor would share her experience and suggest answers.

Roberta also became willing to try new things and follow the suggestions of her sponsor and other members in OA that she trusted. She was willing to work through the twelve steps of the program, one at a time. A major factor that Roberta was realizing from talking to some old-timers in the program was that here is no timetable, because there is no graduation from any of the twelve-step programs.

Speaking of twelve-step programs, she discovered there are at least twelve of them:

ALCOHOLICS ANONYMOUS - A fellowship for those with a desire to stop drinking.

ALANON - A fellowship for family and friends of alcoholics.

ALATEEN - A fellowship for children and teenage family members of alcoholics.

NARCOTICS ANONYMOUS - A fellowship for those with a desire to stop using drugs.

OVEREATERS ANONYMOUS - A fellowship for those with a desire to stop eating compulsively.

ADULT CHILDREN OF ALCOHOLICS - A fellowship for adult children of alcoholics and other dysfunctional families.

CODEPENDENTS ANONYMOUS - A fellowship for those with an inability to maintain functional relationships.

SEXAHOLICS ANONYMOUS - A fellowship for those with a desire to stop their sexually self-destructive thinking and behavior.

S-ANON - A fellowship for those who have friends or family with sexual self-destructive thinking and behavior.

NICOTINE ANONYMOUS - A fellowship for those with a desire to stop smoking.

DUAL DISORDERS ANONYMOUS - A fellowship for those who suffer from mental and emotional difficulties as well as substance abuse problems.

GAMBLERS ANONYMOUS - A fellowship for those with a desire to stop gambling compulsively.

As the years passed for Roberta in the OA program, she began to have a better understanding of the organization and how the Twelve Traditions have sustained this and other twelve-step programs. They are as follows:

"1. Our common welfare should come first; personal recovery depends upon OA unity.
2. For our group purpose there is but one ultimate authority -- a loving God as He may express Himself in our group conscience. Our leaders are but trusted servants; they do not govern.
3. The only requirement for OA membership is a desire to stop eating compulsively.
4. Each group should be autonomous except in matters affecting other groups or OA as a whole.
5. Each group has but one primary purpose -- to carry its message to the compulsive overeater who still suffers.
6. An OA group ought never endorse, finance or lend the OA name to any related facility or outside enterprise, lest problems of money, property and prestige divert us from our primary purpose.
7. Every OA group ought to be fully self-supporting, declining outside contributions.
8. Overeaters Anonymous should remain forever non-professional, but our service centers may employ special workers.
9. OA, as such, ought never be organized: but we may create service boards or committees directly responsible to those they serve.
10. Overeaters Anonymous has no opinion on outside issues; hence the OA name ought never be drawn into public controversy.
11. Our public relations policy is based on attraction rather than promotion; we need always maintain personal anonymity at the level of press, radio, films, television, and other public media of communication.
12. Anonymity is the spiritual foundation of all these traditions, ever reminding us to place principles before personalities."

Roberta read these words of wisdom and thought, if only our federal government could be organized under such traditions, what a wonderful land we would be. The founding fathers of

Alcoholics Anonymous had framed these words over sixty years ago and they have served not only alcoholics but many sick people in the other twelve-step programs.

NETLIVING NOTES:

* Netliving will help enhance your twelve-step program. I've learned that I need people to help me though life's journey.
* Netliving will make you more aware of the assistance that is available for those who suffer. I've learned to have the wisdom to remain teachable.
* Netliving will facilitate your ability to carry the message to those who have these illnesses. I've learned that "No man is an island, no man can stand alone."

CHAPTER FOURTEEN

RECIPE FOR LEISURE

"A faithful friend is a strong defense: and he that hath found such one hath found a treasure."

Apocrypha

It was the first working day of the new year and Richard was sitting in his office planning his days activities. He was human resource manager for a large food processing plant. There was a knock at the door and a large African-American group leader poked his head in the door. He was accompanied by a team leader and two employees and wanted to have a disciplinary discussion with them in Richard's presence.

On the last working day of the year, it was a custom on the second shift for the line mechanic to walk down the line and wish all the production employees, a happy New Year. The mechanic on line six was in the process of passing along his good wishes when he ran into a difficulty -- he was shaking hands with the male employees and kissing the female workers.

When he came to the female who was now sitting in Richard's office, she spit in his face. Since this particular female employee was a lesbian, she objected to being kissed by the mechanic. She was still "fried" about the whole episode and was ready to do battle again.

Fred, the mechanic, on the other hand, was a "macho man" -- he screamed at the top of his voice that, "No goddam dike is going to get away with spitting on me." He continued, "Who knows where her tongue has been and what kind of disease she is carrying around in her mouth." At this point Richard came down on him with both feet. He said, "Fred, you are in big trouble, just sit down and keep your mouth shut." He continued, "When I want to hear from you I will ask, UNDERSTAND."

After hearing both sides of the story, Richard said to the mechanic, "Fred, you were out of line by trying to kiss someone who did not want to be kissed, custom or not." He turned to Judy, the operator and said, "Judy you have been around here long enough to know that spitting on fellow employees is not acceptable, especially in a food processing plant." Then Richard turned to the team leader and said, "Bill, I want you to write both of them up." He continued, "It should be a written warning and indicate that any future violations of company policy of this nature will lead to further, more severe disciplinary action to and including discharge." They both left the office with heads down.

At quitting time Fred stopped by Richard's office to have a few words with him. He apologized for any inconvenience he caused and indicated he had learned his lesson and would not be that stupid again. Switching to some small talk, he asked Richard if he had ever done any cross country skiing. Richard indicated his brother-in-law had just given him a pair of old cross country training skies as a Christmas gift. He had been out every day between Christmas and New Year's Day trying them out. He really liked the feeling of the total peace one experienced out in the woods, with the unblemished white snow and the birds and animals in their natural habitat.

Fred said, "Why don't we go over to the local state park that has cultured ski trails and a nice base of snow and cross country ski next Sunday morning?" Thus began a life-long friendship of enjoying many happy leisure hours, skiing together.

When the winter was over, Richard invited "Mr. Goodwrench", as he fondly called Fred, to try some mountain biking with him. Richard's new friend went to the local cycle shop and bought a ten-speed mountain bike, it was good enough for getting started. Richard himself had begun with a touring bike that had only five speeds, with thin "road" tires. He quickly advanced to a twenty-one speed cross-country bike. This was a combination road and trail bike. It had index shifting and on-board computer. This amazing device reported one's speed, distance traveled, average rate of speed for the trip, and the length of time expended on the overall jaunt.

This netliving experience had been good for both Richard and Fred. It had helped Richard better understand what the employees in the plant were feeling about various company policy changes. On the other hand, it was good experience for the younger man to learn not only new leisure activities but be exposed to a more mature and knowledgeable group of people who were Richard's and Roberta's friends.

As summer rolled around, Richard joined the company golf league along with his friend Mr. Goodwrench. They had requested placement on the same team and were happy when their request was granted. This awesome twosome burned up the course and ended up winning first place in their league that year.

They continued to ride their bikes through the trails within the nearby national forest, usually on weekends. Occasionally, Roberta and some of her girlfriends would join them and they would bring along a picnic lunch. Sometimes these trips were a distance of twenty-five miles. In addition, this team signed up for a "bikeathon" (a twenty-five mile ride) for the American Cancer Society. This meant they had to persuade people to pledge a certain amount of money per mile and then, when the ride was finished, they collected the promised contribution for the local Chapter of the American Cancer Society.

During these rides they met many interesting people, had great times and enjoyed the feeling of well-being and accomplishment it gave them for contributing their efforts to such a worthwhile cause.

Soon the fall became winter and their thoughts turned to snow and cross-country skiing again. This year they had decided to enter a few competitive races to add some excitement to their otherwise drab winter existence. Richard had suggested to his non-skiing friends, who were complaining about the large amount of snow they received on the north coast, to take up skiing so they could anticipate the snowfall with joy.

The date for the Kaiser Permanente "Frost Belt Classic" had been scheduled for February 10th. The "Bonnie Bell Winter Classic" had been planned the week before. Fred and Richard had been training all winter so they were feeling confident about their ability to compete. They decided to enter both races. Their strategy: they would warm-up with the Bonnie Bell race and be ready to go for the gold in the Frost Belt Classic. The latter was the more prestigious of the two. Both races were taking place at the state park the skiers used to practice.

The morning of the Frost Belt Classic, Richard picked up his mechanic friend at an early hour so they would have plenty of time to arrive at the park and prepare their skis with wax. As they were driving along on an icy rural road they noticed an apparent "damsel in distress." Fred (an unmarried guy) motioned for Richard to pull over to see if they could be of help. They did so and found this young lady upset because she had borrowed her daddy's BMW and now it was lying in a ditch, nose down at an odd angle.

The two skiers pushed and shoved and rocked the "ultimate driving machine" with the frightened young girl valiantly behind the wheel. Finally after a half hour of rocking the fine automobile extricated itself from its snowy prison amid much vigorous appreciation expressed by the young woman. Richard said to Fred, "I have a positive feeling about helping her, even though she was too young for you, our good Samaritan act may give us luck in the race."

Richard exceeded his usual conservative speed on the snow-ice slickened roadway, and they arrived at the race site with plenty of time to spare. Richard removed his wax kit from the trunk of his car and began the process of checking the weather conditions so he could determine the proper wax application. The simple test he always used was if you could make a snowball with the snow then above freezing wax was used. If the snow was so light and fluffy it would not make a tight snowball then the below freezing wax was applied to the skies.

Somehow, Richard made a mistake and applied the improper wax on his skis. By the time the race began, however, the weather conditions had changed tremendously and the wax he had put on his skis in error was now perfect for the new conditions.

The race began, and it was something to behold. There were two tracked trails that several hundred skiers were funneled into. These skiers had ski-poles with sharp, knife-like points used to penetrate the icy surface, help keep balance and assist the skier along. These weapons could do heavy damage to an unsuspecting participant.

The conditions had iced up and most of the skiers had either "no-wax" skis, not very effective in icy conditions, or had put on a wax that was designed for wet snow. Richard was moving past all of these struggling skiers, including his special skiing buddy. Richard was not a particularly fast skier, but with the wax he had on his skis he was moving noticeably well, especially on the hills. Richard arrived at the finish line of the ten kilometer race exhausted but triumphant.

When the awards ceremony took place an hour later, Richard was awarded a bronze medal for his age group. Fred reminded him of his earlier comment, "that doing an act of kindness for the stranger stuck at the side of the road may have brought him good luck." For it was pure luck that caused him to win the race that day. Richard said, "I'd rather be lucky than not."

The following week, the two entered the big race (The Frost Belt Classic) and made a good showing, but this time they were not medal winners. Kidding each other, they talked about trying to find some poor motorist stranded along the way to improve their chances of winning.

The following spring Richard received a phone call from an old friend who had been a fellow human resource manager at a company where both formerly worked. This close personal friend had left the human resources field to go into the real estate business with his father in the Washington, D.C. area. "The captain" as we affectionately called him, needed an extra crew member on a forty-five foot sailing sloop he was chartering in the British Virgin Islands. The "sail" was to be for two weeks at the beginning of November.

In secret, Richard had dreamed of such a trip for many years, dating back to his navy days aboard those big gray monster ships. He didn't want to get too excited until he talked it over with his wife. In an instant she was excited for his opportunity, and quickly indicated that while he was away, she would go off to Hilton Head with a girlfriend who had invited her to visit their condo on that renowned island off the North Carolina coast.

When Richard mentioned this "dream trip" to a fellow worker named Ron, who was a training instructor, he asked excitedly, "Can I come along?" He begged Richard to call his real estate friend, the captain, and ask if there was room for him. Reluctantly, Richard made the call and found there were no openings, but the captain indicated he would put Ron on a waiting list.

At that point, Richard did some netliving to investigate taking a quick course on sailing. He discovered the American Red Cross had an introductory course that was beginning in August. Ron, the training instructor, also signed up for the course, a bit of a risk since there was no firm indication he would be a member of the dream trip crew. The two sailors-in-training went faithfully to the lessons every Monday and Wednesday evening for eight weeks. They had "skull sessions" on shore for an hour and then practiced sailing on small sail fish class boats. This was a great experience for the beginners because the boats were small enough to make the process easier to see, thus simplifying the principles of sailing.

Richard was amazed at the power of wind. He was told by the sailing instructor that a sail on a boat is like the wing on an aircraft. The same dynamic principle that causes the plane to lift off the ground when the wind travels across the wing is what happens with a sail. It is not a pushing force but a pulling force, which is how a sailboat can sail almost directly into the wind.

During the last week in September, the dream trip captain called and indicated one of the crew members from California had to cancel for business reasons and now there was a berth for Ron if he was still interested. When Richard informed him of the news he was ecstatic. His preparatory risk-taking had paid off; now he was certified by the American Rd Cross to be a beginning sailor.

November finally came and the two novice sailors boarded a plane and headed for Charlotte Amailia on Saint Thomas Island in the U.S. Virgin Islands. This trip was by way of Washington, D.C., where the other crew members were boarding. They went on to Miami to pick up their direct flight to St. Thomas. It was an exciting adventure for all of them, but especially the newly certified seamen.

There were six members of the crew, including the captain. All the other crew members besides Richard and his friend were experienced sailors. The youngest member of the team was probably the best sailor and owned his own thirty-two foot sloop, a sailboat with one mast and usually two sails (main and jib). This young man, the knowledgeable sailor, was a computer analyst and real sharp. It was reassuring for Richard and Ron to know they had such bright and experienced sailors as part of the crew.

They boarded a ferry that took them from Saint Thomas to Tortola Island in the British Virgin Islands where their charter awaited them. There was a strong contrast between St. Thomas and Tortola. St. Thomas was commercial, whereas Tortola was natural. When the ferry arrived at Tortola, the crew had to take a taxi to Fat Hogs Bay after checking in with the local customs agent. The taxi ride over the mountains, on the left side of the winding road with hairpin turns while traveling at a high rate of speed, was an unnerving experience all by itself.

The first night on the island was spent in a hotel on the waterfront since they could not take possession of their boat until noon the following day. The crew had a wonderful native seafood dinner at the restaurant affiliated with the hotel. They went to bed early, anticipating a busy day. They awoke to roosters loudly announcing the new day amid the many nautical sounds of the waterfront. The crew had a good breakfast of bacon and eggs and was given chart briefings and a walk-through check-out of their seagoing home away from home.

The next ten days brought many exciting adventures along with some memorable difficulties for the crew.

The weather was dominated by sunny days and balmy, warm nights. They had some great sails from island to island and saw many awesome sights. The water was crystal clear and the snorkeling over the storied reefs was a great once-in-a-lifetime experience.

The main difficulty the crew had with this particular boat besides the fact that it did not have a name -- just a number, was the fresh water tanks had hidden leaks that caused the crew to return again and again to port to replenish the supply.

Toward the end of the trip it became clear to Richard that his friend Ron was missing some of his creature comforts. This camping-on-water was definitely not for him. For example, to conserve fresh water the crew took a seawater shower every afternoon. This consisted of jumping off the back of the boat and getting wet, then a fast lather-up with a dish washing detergent, then back into the sea to rinse. Finally, a quart of fresh water was used to rinse the salt and residual soap off. This procedure was pure torture for Ron.

On the last night aboard they were anchored off Fat Hogs Bay and Ron was imploring Richard to take him ashore so he could take a warm, on-shore, fresh water shower. This did not go over well because Richard was in the process of packing his gear for the trip home and he wanted to finish that distasteful task. He finally relented and took his friend ashore to get his warm shower.

On the return trip to the sloop, Richard reminded his friend that he was to tie up the dinghy since he was the mate on this venture. Richard went back below decks to finish his packing. A few minutes later, he heard a loud commotion on the deck above him. The dinghy was gone and was nowhere to be found. Ron was upset because he was the one who tied it up. He began yelling the he had lost his dinghy but no one from the shore could hear him. The captain called on the radio and asked for some help from anyone who heard the radio broadcast.

After what seemed like hours of futile yelling from the fantail, Ron was almost hysterical. Someone mentioned the cost of a dinghy and outboard engine would be at least a thousand dollars to replace. Finally, a young girl's voice came over the radio. She was an Australian and she said, "Hello, I copy your message and will come to your rescue when my mates return from shore."

About a half hour later, she showed up with one of her crew and they took a worried Ron on a search for the missing dinghy. They had almost immediate success and the smiling novice sailor was promising eternal gratitude. He came aboard the sloop and explained to the captain that when he tied the dinghy he only used "a five-minute knot" since he knew the rest of the crew was going ashore within five minutes. This prompted several other members of the crew including Richard to write parodies of the now infamous five-minute knot. The next morning the whole island knew of the loss of the dinghy. Nautical news always traveled fast, especially out in the islands. Soon, the crew was jokingly referring to the five-minute knot every time a line needed to be secured .

This fantastic island cruising venture was only the beginning of many annual trips for Richard, the captain and the crew. However it was the last time Ron ever stepped foot on a sailboat.

On the next trip, Richard brought his son along on a visit to the Tabogos in the Bahama Islands. This was a rewarding father and son project. The agreement was that during the duration of the trip the two would just be mates and not father and son. They wore identical shirts and shorts when they went ashore. Richard and his son shared the same cabin and head. They were a two-man team when it came to work details. The same was true for fun experiences like snorkeling or exploring deserted islands.

One day they were on laundry duty which entailed taking all the laundry in the dinghy and finding someone on the nearest island to wash it. They were anchored off Green Turtle Cay so they decided to dinghy over to New Plymouth which was a port on the island. There they asked about a laundromat but found out there was none in the whole area. Then someone directed them to the Green Turtle Shipyard which had shut down. Richard's son talked to the post mistress and she gave him the name and address of a lady who sometimes does laundry. They walked through a narrow path to a shabby looking house but she wasn't home. Back in town they found a lady named Fanny who agreed to wash two bags of clothes and have them ready by 5 PM for $20.

Richard and his son went over to the New Plymouth Lounge and had a few beers. They met a Jimmy Buffet type who had been island hopping for four years. He had a political science degree and knew much about our political system and was interesting to talk with.

They moved on to the Green Turtle Historical Museum. Richard's son felt the $3 admission charge was too steep so he ended paying for both of them . The tour of Mr. Robert Lowe's home was educational and it killed the better part of the afternoon. They decided since the customs office was closed they should head up to pick up the laundry. Their directions were to go to the top of the hill near the "Rooster's Roost," which is a sports bar.

Richard and his son walked passed it the first time because it looked kind of rough. Then they returned and a nice young black fellow showed them where Fanny the laundry lady lived. They were about thirty minutes early and the clothes were not dry yet. They walked back to the Roost and ordered up a couple of beers and sat down next to the crew from the "Flipper." There was a young couple from Jacksonville and two other mates from Palm Springs. One of these crew members was negotiating with the bartender over a carved wooden parrot that was on a shelf behind the bar. He asked Richard what he thought it was worth and he said it looked like at least $100 worth of man hours went into producing such a fine work of art. Finally he bought it for $35. Richard and his son walked over to the bar and saw the great American bald eagle. They were ready to pick up the laundry so they had little time to negotiate. Richard offered the bartender $50 because he wanted $80 and agreed to sell it for $55.

They took a picture of "Samson" the artist who carved both birds and left with his best wishes. He indicated the wood he used is a cousin to mahogany and the natives call it "tamarind." When they finally arrived at Fanny's home she informed them the laundry had not dried and they would have to wait until morning and return. When they arrived back at "Meggy" the rest of the crew was green with envy over the beautiful art treasure that Richard had acquired. The two spent many hours together and were much closer as a result of this adventuresome experience.

Richard's friend, Fred, the mechanic joined the crew for three annual cruises and learned much about sailing and snorkeling. He began with a strong fear of water but gradually overcame it when he learned to swim. By the second year, the crew had him diving from a platform on the stern of the sloop.

Richard was convinced his life and the lives of his family and friends had been enriched by the many leisure activities experienced as a direct result of applying the principles and practical doctrines of netliving.

NETLIVING NOTES:

* Netliving will enhance your leisure time pursuits. I've learned that sharing fun experiences with others doubles the enjoyment.
* Netliving will open up new and exciting adventures. I've learned that feeling good about myself is the most basic requirement of happiness; next comes the friendship and conversation of a few select companions.
* Netliving is sharing life's experiences unselfishly with others. I've learned that defects mixed in with fine qualities make up the total personalities of those who are dear to me.

CHAPTER FIFTEEN

THE BATTLE OF THE SEXES

"Thoughtfulness for others, generosity, modesty and self-respect are the qualities which make a real gentleman or lady."

Thomas Huxley (1825-1895)

From the first days of early childhood memory Roberta was conscious of a level of rivalry between her brother Richard and herself. Being twins did not make the situation between brother and sister any less competitive. Roberta always tried to match Richard in physical sports and worked strenuously at being as physically fit as he was.

Roberta was a better student than Richard because she was willing to invest hours of studying while he chose to spend the same hours playing ball or fishing. Academic competition was encouraged by their parents. This caused many arguments between the sister and brother in their home; at times these confrontations became heated.

As she grew older, Roberta's competitive spirit was transferred from her brother to all other members of the male gender. Her belief that she could do anything equally as well as a boy was planted deep within her brain and spirit. This quality appealed to some young men, while others were repulsed by what appeared to be an over-aggressive personality.

At this point in her life she had not learned the adage, "men are from Mars, and women are from Venus." One of Roberta's high school teachers attempted to explain that boys and girls think and feel differently. This sensitive teacher explained that trying to ignore these differences only creates more confusion, frustration and conflict between the sexes.

The teacher explained to Roberta's class that the human brain has two hemispheres. The left hemisphere of the brain is used for language skills while the right side of the brain is used for spatial, problem-solving skills. She pointed out that boys have a tendency to use one side of the brain at a time. On the other hand, girls have a tendency to use both sides of the brain simultaneously.

That concept explained why, when Roberta came rushing home with a crisis and her brother quickly offered a solution, she became disappointed and reacted negatively. Rather, she wanted Richard to listen as she outlined her problem and then function in combination with her as she systematically developed a proposed tactical resolution. Roberta needed a sounding board as she processed information using both sides of her brain. Richard was using the right side of his brain to reach an immediate solution of her problem based on very little data or criteria input.

When Roberta tried to explain her complex position, her brother, feeling rejected, disappeared somewhere in a huff, "to be alone" where he would quietly attempt to understand the female-oriented behavior of his dear sister. Richard would have to ponder for a while just how he felt about what his sister had just told him. Looking at the situation from another perspective, Roberta was able to feel, think and speak all at the same time.

The health teacher also pointed out that boys cope with stress differently than girls do. In pre-historic times when a hunter failed to slay the deer or the number of rabbits he wanted, he shifted his attention to less demanding hunting tasks in order to cope with the stress of not providing adequately for those dependent on him. He would go fishing or root gathering, as these pursuits required less effort, he could handle them successfully and it made him forget that he had missed the preferable food animals.

School boys are traditionally successful at temporarily forgetting that they did not earn A's because they didn't study enough. They come to depend on hobbies, sports and other activities which distract them from the disappointment of not accomplishing the more important academic goals.

Competitive sports allow a young male to redirect and channel his aggressiveness. Physical activities enable him to expend his frustration at not being able to solve real-world problems. As boys mature into men, they move on to playing tennis and golf, cross country hiking, sail boating, hunting, deep sea fishing, etc.

Roberta was told these are perfect distractions which allow men to relax through doing. Often men feel much more at ease being together and occasionally talking if they are also doing something out in the open, as in playing the game of golf.

Alternatively, the teacher pointed out that girls and women do not need such distraction. They are absolutely contented to bond relationships by sharing their feelings and thoughts often through long, private conversations. Another point Roberta learned from this perceptive teacher is that modern day TV gazing by both boys and men is the cavemen's equivalent of sitting silently in a circle while gazing into the blazing embers of a fire. Fire gazing is the most ancient and potent of male stress-reducers.

For the rest of her life Roberta would remember these teachings regarding the different thinking processes of men and women and would learn to use that knowledge to her advantage.

As time passed and Roberta eventually entered the business world, she was well aware of the workings of the so called "good old boy network" by which men help one another climb the corporate ladder. She was also aware of the "glass ceiling" which impedes women who strive to reach the highest rungs of the corporate ladder. Many capable women have worked their way up the business ladder of success only to plateau at a level where they can clearly see, but not quite attain, the top.

Roberta found it interesting that, historically, most men confine their netliving activity to their workplace and career activity while women, for the most part, have always netlived in their daily personal lives. Men in general seem to be too "macho" to share what is bothering them. They would rather tough it out alone, keeping the pain all to themselves. Most women will freely share their feelings with others and in the process feel better for the experience while often gaining valuable insight and assistance in the situation or problem.

Roberta believed that a blend of these two approaches would be a benefit for everyone involved.

While attending a convention hosted by the National Association of Investments Clubs, Roberta discovered that the average, all-female investment club had earned an annual return of about 17.9 percent over several years. That compares with 15.6 percent for all-male clubs in the same time period. Clubs with both male and female members earned an appealing average annual return of 17.3 percent.

Roberta was amazed to learn that about seventy percent of NAIC investment club members are women, up from just ten percent in 1960. A book about investment clubs, written by the Beardstown Ladies Investment Club, helped spread the idea's popularity. Here we observe another fascinating example of netliving in action.

Also at the convention were "do-it-yourself investors" who spoke about using the public library and the fantastic world of cyberspace -- the internet. "Own a Share of America" is their motto. More than half a million Americans have joined investment clubs that belong to the NAIC, part of the phenomenon in which sophisticated investment advice is spreading from the trading floor to the living room.

Roberta read a magazine article about a group of Women CEOs who set up a netliving association to help each other. This California group covered subjects such as "how to learn to sail," since sailing is said to be the preferred leisure activity of venture capital people who enjoy funding the operations of small companies. "To sail is to schmooze ... is to get funded ... is to be successful."

Another member of the group reported her venture capital group liked to golf. She wanted help at the driving range and on the links. There was a show of hands and e-mail addresses were exchanged. Words such as "valuation," "prototype" and "unassisted sales" were sprinkled liberally throughout conversations. This was of strong interest to Roberta. She read on with interest.

One of the members said, "We're a small group and there are few women CEO's. I have no peers. One of the best things for me is that there's a place I feel I can go where I can talk openly about issues. You could never have a similar group of male CEO's . They wouldn't share their ideas, their weaknesses and their fears. We women share our problems, whereas men tend to gloat and tell you only about their victories."

Reading this article gave Roberta some great ideas for her business experience. Although she was not a CEO at the time, that position was not beyond her dreams. She also realized that building relationships is vital to business growth, whether you own a small business, work in sales or perform a visible function within a large corporation.

Today people need to know you, or know someone else who knows you well, before they will buy your products or services. These professional relationships provide necessary business referrals. Roberta had a problem when it came to trusting men both in a business setting and in the personal arena. She shared this challenge with many women in their relationships with men.

The only man she felt comfortable discussing this "trust issue" with was her brother, Richard. They had many long discussions about the trust between women and men both in the workplace and in everyday life. Richard was a good sounding board and had some of the same concerns with women that Roberta had with men.

Roberta reminded herself to keep opening up when feeling disappointed is difficult. She found that the secret to trust is not to expect the male to be perfect, but to believe that you are growing in the skills that help you help him give you what you need.

In such a trusting environment, men feel free to speak their minds, knowing that they will get their "day in court." They may not get their way, but they will be heard. Roberta felt this was a reasonable approach and determined to practice the following techniques in her relationships with men: Communicate wishes clearly, delegate tasks and responsibilities, permit freedom and latitude in actions, encourage risk taking, treat failures as "lessons learned," make timely decisions, ask for feedback, and take action as indicated on the feedback received.

Roberta was very much aware that gender disputes, if not handled properly, could get ugly and lead to sexual discrimination or sexual harassment. The 1991 confirmation hearings for Supreme Court Justice Clarence Thomas heightened Americans' awareness of differing perceptions about what constitutes sexual harassment. Officially, sexual harassment is a violation of Title VII of the Civil Rights Act of 1964.

According to federal guidelines issued to interpret and implement Title VII, Roberta learned that sexual harassment is defined as unwelcome sexual advances, requests for sexual favors, and other verbal or physical conduct of a sexual nature when such conduct creates a hostile or offensive work environment. If the conduct is unwelcome and occurs with sufficient frequency to create an abusive work environment, the employer is responsible for changing the environment by warning, reprimanding and even firing the guilty harasser.

Roberta was also aware that because an employer has the power to reprimand or fire an offender, an employer is legally liable for the sexual harassment acts of its employees, whether or not the employer knows they are occurring. However, liability is reduced if an employer has a clear, well-publicized policy forbidding harassment and follows up immediately on complaints.

Most instances involve a man sexually harassing a woman. However, sexual harassment can also be a woman harassing a man, a woman harassing a woman, or a man harassing a man. Sexual harassment adversely affects everyone. For the organization, it can result in lower morale thus lower productivity, increased costs for hiring and training new employees, significant legal costs and fines as well as poor public relations. For the workers, sexual harassment can cause emotional and physical pain, less effective job performance and personal and financial problems.

There is no excuse for sexual harassment in this enlightened era of the nineties. In general, the law clearly states that any unwelcome sexual conduct or attention constitutes sexual harassment if the employee's job depends upon the response. For example: a supervisor implies that keeping your job depends on "sharing a room" on a business trip, "dating" customers, or having an "affair."

Roberta was aware that when salary increases or promotions depended on a positive response in such a situation, sexual harassment was taking place.

In netliving with her professional peers, Roberta learned that sexual harassment can take many forms, some rather subtle. Sexual harassment can be exhibited by verbal threats or insults, offensive or suggestive comments, messages containing disguised sexual content, pressure for dates, outright propositions, offensive cartoons or jokes or teasing, extending out even to whistles or catcalls. She also found sexual harassment can be expressed non-verbally through suggestive gestures or even looks(winks, licking the lips, rolling the eyes, staring or leering, etc.) , or displaying risqué posters, photos or drawings of a sexual suggestive nature.

On the extreme end, sexual harassment leads to physical acts of violent abuse and assault such as rape or attempted rape, cornering or trapping, pinching, grabbing, patting, forceful touching, violent hugging or kissing. Roberta also found that the perception of sexual harassment depends upon how the person being harassed is affected and NOT on the harassers's intent.

Roberta appealed to all the employees in her organization to help prevent sexual harassment by maintaining a professional attitude at all times, combined with a thorough knowledge of the company's policy defining sexual harassment.

Consider your attitudes about sexual harassment. Ask yourself how you would feel if you, a relative or a friend were harassed. What would you do? Set a positive example by treating everyone with whom you come in contact with the same respect you want in return. Let others know you expect this same treatment from them. Talk with your co-workers about sexual harassment, get it out in the open, air it out, be a good listener.

"Be aware of your words and actions and what goes on around you," Roberta urged the other team members. Avoid making assumptions that "practical jokes," "friendly gestures or comments," etc., are harmless, and don't really constitute offensive conduct. Find out if the act really is inoffensive to all concerned. Quite often you will find a comment is not viewed the same way by everyone. Think before making personal comments or even asking personal questions. Inquire of your conscience, could such comment or question make the other person feel uncomfortable? Don't go along with the "crowd." or accept behavior that may be offensive to someone alone and outside the "group." Make your feelings known to those around you. Ask that the offensive behavior be stopped immediately. Be supportive of people who're being sexually harassed, offer them your friendship and assistance completely on their terms. Remind them that sexual harassment is never the victim's fault, and encourage them to take action. Offer to be a witness if necessary.

Roberta was assertive when addressing a gathering of employees. She provided them with some general guidelines: Confront the harasser and clearly state that the behavior offends you and that you want it to stop. Keep a record of the event. Write down what happened, where and when it happened and who witnessed it. A written account is important because memories can be unreliable. Talk to your supervisor if the harassment doesn't stop. Present your record of the incident and produce a witness if possible. Keep a record of what your supervisor says and does about the complaint. Talk directly to your supervisor's boss if your supervisor is the harasser.

Roberta went on to point out that there are other resources for help if your supervisor doesn't take appropriate action or if the harassment continues. You may contact an affirmative action officer, a grievance committee, an employee support group or an employee advocacy group.

Lastly, consider filing a formal complaint. For additional information contact these sources of relief: Equal Employment Opportunity Commission, the state attorney general's office, the district attorney, state or city department of human or civil rights. All of these are listed in the telephone directory.

Many employees mentioned the frightening news reports concerning the situation in the blatant sexual harassment in the military establishment and even the internationally embarrassing sexual misconduct of the President of the United States. Roberta again stressed the importance of the tactical steps mentioned above.

On the other hand, investigators of alleged sexual harassment complaints must take a very balanced approach when looking into such charges so that justice is served equally for all concerned.

NETLIVING NOTES:

* Netliving will improve your ability to communicate with the opposite sex. I've learned that no matter how thin you slice it, there are always two sides.
* Netliving will help women improve their business and financial status. I've learned that women can have their "good old gal network."
* Netliving will improve your awareness of sexual harassment and the positive action available to you to prevent sexual harassment. I've learned to ask myself how I would feel if a relative or friend were harassed?

CHAPTER SIXTEEN

FOR PROBLEM SOLVING

"The best way out is always through."

Robert Frost
(1874-1963)

As a young boy growing up in a rural area, Richard used his netliving skills to solve problems because there were very few professional service shops available, and even less money to spend for such services. The need for bike repairs took him across the street to a neighbor who was three years older and was the recognized local expert on repairing bicycles. Richard spent hours learning how to change a tire, adjust the brakes and replace a broken chain.

As Richard aged and acquired more expensive "toys," this practice of netliving with family and friends to solve repair and maintenance problems continued. His 1940 Chrysler was relatively rust free but left much to be desired, mechanically speaking.

Prior to owning the auto Richard had netlived with one of his newspaper route customers to earn a few driving lessons. Richard agreed to mow his instructor's lawn in exchange for lessons. This is an arrangement commonly know as "bartering." To Richard's knowledge at that time there were no formal driving schools. Richard's parents had never owned an auto, so he had to reach out and netlive with someone who had the time and ability to teach him how to drive.

When it came to repairing the "tank" as Richard's dark green '40 Chrysler was affectionately known, his driving coach was helpful there too. As the owner of a 1941 Dodge, he was familiar with many of the comparable components used under the hood in both cars. Richard was able to "piggy-back" on mechanical repairs as they became necessary because his instructor "had been there and done that" in most cases of repair. Also, a friend from West Virginia who worked as a mechanic at his uncle's auto dealership and owned a '41 DeSoto proved helpful. Because the cars were similar in design and in performance, he too helped repair the "tank" when it needed special attention, which was quite often.

This type of netliving carried over to the maintenance of Richard's first home, and worked so well that it became a part of his subsequent home ownership. He and his wife were typical young homeowners. They had scraped together all the money they could get their hands on to provide the down payment. The monthly mortgage payments kept them strapped financially. When something broke or wore out they questioned family and friends to obtain the cheapest solution possible to the necessary fix-up problem.

On the other hand, once Richard and his wife developed particular domestic skills, they would freely pass them along to other young couples in need. They became proficient at painting, although they learned rather quickly that it would never become their favorite activity.

They had several netliving friends who were stronger in sophisticated areas such as electrical wiring and complicated plumbing repairs, and these they called on for their expertise. One such friend was an electrician in the plant where Richard worked. He helped install ceiling paddle fans in several of their homes over the years.

The saying "Two heads are better than one" had always held true for Richard, especially when it came to problem solving. One boyhood dream was to own a summer home near a lake.

This dream did not look as though it would ever become reality when he married a girl from New York City. When they were courting, she promised she would never ask him to settle down in the city if he did not expect her to live in a small rural town.

Richard argued that a summer home used five or six months out of the year was a different matter from the agreed arrangement, so he planned to make it happen. Through netliving with his brother-in-law he began looking at hundred-acre farms in rural areas. This action panicked his wife, and one summer while they were staying at a rented cabin for a week, he found the answer to his dream.

On the bulletin board at the local Laundromat Richard spotted an ad for a two-acre plot of land with a 60 x 12 foot mobile home located on it. A woman who noticed his interest in the ad urged him to go across the state line where she claimed the property costs were much cheaper. He took her advice and later, while on their way to the local amusement park, Richard casually mentioned the conversation to his wife. He pulled into the mobile home sales lot and asked for the owner.

The owner was away from the lot but the individual on duty encourage them to inspect any of the trailers on the lot. Patty, Richard's wife, was impressed by all the units but found the hunter-green and white trailer to be the most practical for their family's needs. The person on duty could not quote prices, and Richard knew his wife's choice would probably be the most expensive unit on the lot anyhow.

The family climbed back into the station wagon and proceeded to enjoy the day riding the roller coaster and other scary rides at their favorite amusement park. On the return trip they passed the mobile home lot and stopped to see if the owner was on duty. They found he was there this time. They hit it off so well that the owner took them to see a new development where he was just beginning to clear the land. The property, adjacent to a deer preserve, would be named after the developer's daughter. Richard and his family immediately fell in love with the location and were ready to make a deal. Patty was much less reluctant to the project when she learned that the trailer she had selected was the lowest priced on the lot.

Since the owner was eager to have a model in the new development right away, he was willing to sell the first home site for a very reasonable price. Richard and his family were so excited they could not sleep that night. They wanted the place but at the time it was a "push" for them financially, and owning the property promised budget difficulties. They went home and thought about if for the next week and did some netliving about the decision with friends and family. Richard's mother-in-law saved the day with an offer to help with the down payment. The final decision was to go ahead and purchase the mobile home and the two acres of land.

At the time, Richard and his wife felt they would probably own the place for a period of about ten years. They believed the children, and even themselves, would be tired of it by then and the mobile home would have deteriorated to such a point by that time that they would not want to deal with the maintenance. However, years later the vacation home is standing tall and is still used frequently by the children, grandchild, brothers and sisters and their friends as well as by Richard and his wife.

Another interesting problem that was solved through netliving was connected with this summer home. The mobile home was located about three blocks from a large man-made lake which came into existence during the Great Depression of the 1930's. In the early thirties President Franklin D. Roosevelt passed legislation that created the PWA (Public Works Act). Many recreational facilities that we enjoy today were created through the efforts of the he PWA.

Old timers around the lake told Richard of the unemployed men who came in their white dress shirts with neckties carrying picks and shovels ready to go to work to build the dam that created this wonderful inland lake. Their labor resulted in a beautiful lake, two and a half miles wide and seven miles long with twenty five miles of splendid recreational shoreline.

Being located close to the lake had many benefits but also created a unique problem for Richard and his family in the form of big, hungry mosquitoes. They were found everywhere in the summer and at times made life seriously uncomfortable. Richard had heard a speech at one of his Toastmasters meetings that gave him an answer to this problem --BATS.

Listening to the speech Richard learned that even tiny bats perform a very important function in nature's food chain. On a daily basis they eat their own weight in insects, which of course includes the dreaded mosquito. One solution to the mosquito problem at the vacation cabin would be to have a group of bats move onto that otherwise pleasant property.

This was easier said than done. Richard methodically approached the problem by researching the habits of bats, applying the principles of netliving to this otherwise mundane pursuit. He found he had known very little about bats. Among other things, Richard was amazed to find that they like to hang upside down in dark places during the daylight hours. The typical habitat is an old barn with some of the boards missing that allows that bats an easy way to come and go. This posed a problem as there were no old barns located on the vacation property.

Richard talked about needing the bats so often that the next Christmas a family member surprised him with a prefabricated bat chalet as a gift. He was excited and couldn't wait for spring so he could mount the home-for-bats in one of the tall oak trees at the vacation home.

Spring came and Richard and his son set out to install the bat chalet. They selected a prime secluded spot about twenty-five feet above the ground in a large tree. They decided the bats would feel comfortable being that far away from humans and other predators. Then they waited awhile and then they waited some more. Two years passed without any sign of the small brown variety of bat said to be common to the locale. The tiny little creatures steadfastly refused to arrive. The mosquitoes continued their attack in force without any let up. After so long a time, Richard grew increasingly impatient.

He finally approached a park ranger at one of the nature museums and told him about the bats refusing the free housing. The accommodating ranger smiled when he heard the complaint and said, "No problem, we deal with this situation on a regular basis. First you find a nice old barn in the neighborhood and go into it with a flashlight at dusk. Shine the light up into the rafters and notice where the bats are hanging. Directly below them, as you might expect, you will find their droppings. Using a small scoop or shovel, collect some of the droppings and seal them in a ziplock plastic bag. Then, the final step is to place these recovered droppings on the roof of your bat house."

On the heels of this advice, Richard and his son started out one warm summer evening in search of bats and their precious excrement. The first barn they found had to be excluded since the barn was not high enough to be a safe haven for bats. By the time they located a suitable barn, it was too dark and the bats were off somewhere enjoying their nocturnal insect feast.

On the way back to their summer home, Richard spotted a likely looking barn. They noticed what appeared to be the farmer who owned it standing outside. Richard approached the farmer while his son followed along with the flashlight, carrying a large size ziplock bag. The farmer turned out to be as accommodating as the park ranger had been. He took them to a smaller garage type building which had wooden walls covered by sheets of rusty metal. The farmer pried loose one of the old sheets and disclosed a large supply of bat guano. He used his shovel to dig it out and filled the large ziplock bag to the brim. The droppings did not appear as Richard and his son had expected. They had the mistaken notion that the bat guano would resemble bird droppings common to us all, while in fact the material in the plastic bag was quite similar to the often found calling cards left behind by mice.

They thanked the helpful farmer and headed triumphantly back to camp armed with enough bat guano to do the job and then some. The other members of their group could not believe Richard and his son had actually accomplished their strange mission. Nevertheless, the dry droppings still had to get to the top of the bat chalet and remain there long enough to attract some bats.

The next morning Richard awoke with a creative solution to introduce the bat guano to the roof of the bat chalet. He went into the nearby wooded area and cut a small sapling that had a nice v-shaped fork at its top. He cut an end off an empty aluminum beverage can and punched a skewer through the middle of the can. Next he taped the ends of the skewer to the tips of the forked branch. Then he taped several lengths of long thin boards together and to the sapling. He mixed well water with the droppings to make a paste which he placed in the can. Very carefully he performed the feat of raising the pole above the bat house twenty-five feet up in the tree, and by rubbing the beverage can on the limbs of the oak tree above the roof of the bat chalet, he caused the can to tip and spread its contents on either side of the peaked roof of the long-vacant bat house.

Within one week the bat house was inhabited by several dozen small brown bats and soon there was nary a mosquito in evidence on the vacation property.

While on vacation in Florida one winter, Richard experienced another netliving example of "listening for problems and hearing solutions." He was in a K-Mart store looking for some automobile supplies when he noticed some senior citizens sitting at a card table advertising a benefit dance at the local Elks Lodge to be held the following Saturday. When he read that the benefit was for a little girl suffering from liver cancer at the age of three, his heart went out to her and her depressed family.

Richard approached the women and asked about the little girl. They told him she had been diagnosed with cancer the previous October and since then had endured five rounds of chemotherapy. This rare liver cancer, technically known as hepatoblastoma, was fifteen centimeters in size when first discovered. since the therapy the cancer had shrunk to six centimeters and the lesions had decreased from eighteen to eight.

Armed with this optimistic information, Richard not only bought a ticket but encouraged about a dozen other residents to attend. They not only enjoyed the dance but helped raise $4,500 for the trust fund for the brave little girl's ongoing medical bills. The netliving process that Richard and many others employed to help this stricken family was deeply appreciated.

Like Jimmy Stewart's character (George Bailey) said in Richard's favorite film, *IT'S A WONDERFUL LIFE,* "No man is poor who has friends."

NETLIVING NOTES:

* Netliving will help your problem solving skills. I've learned the first step in solving a problem is defining it.

* Netliving will enable you to "Listen for problems and hear opportunities." I've learned life is full of challenges that are disguised as problems.
* Netliving will offer you the opportunity to help others. I've learned that service to others helps my self-esteem.

CHAPTER SEVENTEEN

TO COMPREHEND DIVERSITY

"Be not angry that you cannot make others as you wish them to be, since you cannot make yourself as you wish to be."

Thomas A. Kempis

Growing up in a small town, Roberta encountered a total of two African-Americans during her formative years. These were the Parson brothers who were very nice, young, black men. The older brother was a formal person and sedate. The younger brother was gregarious and fun loving. One young man grew up to become a priest, the other followed the path of his father and became a businessman.

Roberta's age put her in the class between the Parson brothers. However, in a school of less than three hundred students, everyone knew everyone else.

For Roberta, these young people from a completely diverse culture fascinated her. She studied about slavery and the Civil War. These lessons provided an academic background, but the Parson brothers were living evidence the history books sought to describe. She would spend hours after school at the gang's favorite spot asking questions and rapping with these boys of a different culture.

Roberta's parents had immigrated from Ireland and were ethnocentric about what they considered the "Irish Race." They were Irish-Catholics and that lifestyle was the center of their universe. Outsiders were considered second class citizens at best. This simple but strong message had been passed on to Roberta -- "When you grow up you will marry an Irish-Catholic young man." As a child, Roberta's aunt and uncle, who lived nearby, had a great influence on her "Irishness." Her aunt taught her to say her prayers in "The Gaelic," the native Irish tongue.

Holidays were dominated by Irish style singing and dancing, especially in celebration of St. Patrick's Day.

Roberta's parents were not as narrow minded as her aunt and uncle, but there was always a strong preference for things Irish. Roberta attended Catholic elementary school and was influenced strongly by the Sisters of St. Joseph, who were predominantly of Irish descent.

The parish pastor was a big, red-faced Irishman, so the influence was carried over from the home to the school and church. The pastor influenced even Roberta's college choice. With his blessing she chose a college run by nuns.

The Parson brothers were the first persons Roberta had met who were from a completely different culture. She had many friends who were Italian, Polish or Slovenian, but none of these were of a completely different race.

Roberta's next encounter with a "foreign" culture came when her parents decided to participate in a student exchange program through a local university. They signed up to sponsor a student from Bombay, India. When the young man arrived in this country they also adopted his friend, whose sponsoring family had abandoned the program.

The two Indian students landed in the frigid country of North America wearing open sandals and light weight tropical clothing. The first thing Roberta's mother did was take them to a department store to purchase sturdy shoes and heavier clothing. Thus their first experience with snow was a little less shocking than it might have been.

These dark skinned exchange students were also a source of education for Roberta's extended family. On Thanksgiving day the two students joined Roberta's family for the traditional turkey meal. They were puzzled by Roberta's grandfather's pleasant question regarding the name of their "tribe." When it was explained to the old gentleman that they weren't "American Indians," everyone enjoyed a good laugh.

As the two students progressed through their masters degree program and continued on to study for doctorate degrees, they continued to visit Roberta and her family. They spoke of their classes in computers, economics and business. Upon completion of their doctorate programs, both young men returned to India to marry the young Indian women previously chosen for them by their parents. Roberta and her family found this arrangement unusual and thus shocking in the modern age.

Upon returning to the United States a few months later with their new brides they began a new chapter of discovery and fun. One couple was serious, keeping mostly to themselves; the male was busy launching his career and setting up their modest apartment.

On the other hand, the other couple jumped into their new life in the land of abundance. The beautiful new bride was eager to join Roberta's mother on a shopping spree. Armed with the magic of "his" credit card, they set out to select a winter wardrobe. There was instant bonding between Roberta's mother and the young bride. They were like mother and daughter laughing and joking about saving money by finding great bargains in this wonderful land where a tiny plastic card can do so much.

Time passed; eventually the birth of a child brought relatives from India. As the families came together to share the joy, Roberta learned about many Indian customs and about the Hindu religion. It was a great time for both families. Roberta was getting ready to go off to college and this young family was beginning to grow.

Although Roberta had never heard the term "diversity" until the nineties, she had been practicing diversity principles through netliving all her life. She was living the values her parents had taught and displayed by example. Her father used to tell her often, "Roberta, always treat other people the way they want to be treated. Put yourself in the other person's place and ask, 'Is this the way I would treat myself?'"

Roberta chose a small Catholic women's educational institution which had the unique distinction of being the first college in the United States to design its curriculum and method of teaching to match the learning style of women. Most colleges and universities, having been founded by men, had developed courses designed to accommodate male models of learning.

Roberta's college integrated both sides of the brain in a collaborative learning style.

Unfortunately, this wonderful institution of higher learning was too regional to offer much opportunity for netliving toward diversity. Although there were a few European exchange students there were not many widely different cultures represented.

Upon graduation from college, Roberta followed a supervisor's suggestion and registered for a Dale Carnegie Speech course. In this class she met a Japanese-American. As a Korean War veteran, he spoke to Roberta and others about his feelings regarding the treatment of his family during World War II. He shared information about the Japanese culture and how it differs greatly from that of the western world. His people were primarily concerned about losing "face" and would not directly challenge anyone they came in contact with fearful that they should lose this "face" on their account. The lesson she learned proved invaluable for Roberta as she came in contact with other Asian people.

While in graduate school Roberta became interested in the plight of the older person surviving in our society. The subject of her master's thesis was "Planning for an Aging Workforce." Through her research efforts Roberta came in contact with some wonderful people. Among these advocates for older people were several African-Americans and this exposure, plus the contacts she had been making at work, gave her insight into their culture.

Two black women (Anna Brown and Edwardina Riggins) stand out as wonderful examples of people who started in rough circumstances and endured to be courted by presidential candidates. Ewardina had been born of a black mother and a white father and was not accepted by either race. She was abandoned and left at the steps of a convent. The nuns raised her to adulthood and then she went out into the world to make a difference for the "little people." She is currently in her nineties and still going strong. She was visited by candidates Clinton and Gore during the 1996 presidential election campaign and she told the, "If you want to kiss me, kiss me." But she also told them,

"You all better remember us frail, elderly people because there are getting to be a lot of us now."

More than thirty years before, when she was in her late fifties, she began her spirited, tireless crusade as an activist and advocate for senior citizens in the inner city. She was on a first-name basis with several senators and a number of congressmen as well as presidents and vice-presidents of the country and of many large corporations.

The other African-American women, Anna Brown was an outstanding advocate for older people and headed up the Department of Aging in a major midwestern city. She had been involved in many programs to feed and handle the medical needs of older Americans.

Roberta volunteered to serve with these interesting ladies on an aging advocacy committee that looked out for the needs of older people. She learned about diversity by netliving with members of this committee made up of people from widely different backgrounds.

On the job Roberta worked in an organization that had a workforce composed of forty percent of employees from minority groups. She became involved in developing the company's diversity program.

The formal Diversity Awareness training program was developed over a period of eighteen months with the help of some expert consultants. The program was designed to assist employees in becoming aware of ways in which they discriminate against, judge, or isolate others. In this program the term "protected class" referred to groups of people such as African-Americans, Native Americans, Hispanics, Asians, women, older workers, people with disabilities and other minorities in general.

Through netliving with other companies, Roberta found that many were in the same place as her company. They had always tried to treat everyone the same but had not formalized that practice. Many of them had mission statements that read something like this:

"The company is committed to creating, managing and valuing diversity in the workplace and providing a climate where all employees are given the opportunity to achieve their full potential while in pursuit of our corporate strategic objectives."

In talking to various companies some of the questions she asked them and their answers were as follows:

1) Describe your business objectives for your diversity initiatives.

   * To develop and implement programs, policies, and benefits to support the needs of employees.
   * To develop ongoing assessment tools to evaluate employee needs and attitudes.
   * To develop diversity initiatives as part of the corporate strategic plan.
   * To clearly understand the dynamics of our changing workforce along with the business reasons for diversity.
   * To break the concept of diversity down into "real life" situations so people can recognize behaviors and work with more information and understanding.
   * To foster open and honest communication.
   * To create respectful and productive relationships with all kinds of people.

2) Describe your organization's Diversity Policies.

   EDUCATION
   * Orientation for all new employees
   * On-site workshops for business units
   * Management Training

   DIVERSITY RECRUITING
   * Job Fairs
   * Minority College Relations
   * Community/National Organizations
   * Job Banks

   COMMUNICATIONS
   * Diversity defined in published items

- * Publications/advertisements in recruiting magazines
- * Collaboration with community groups
- * Participation in Surveys.

3) Describe your organization's Diversity Practices.

- * Alternative Work Schedules - compressed Workweek, Job Sharing, Part Time Work, Work-at-Home, Flextime
- * Paid Absence Days - Three days off for personal/family needs.
- * Leave of Absences
- * Child/Elder Care Resource and Referral Service
- * Dependent and Health Care Reimbursement Accounts
- * Employee Assistance Program
- * Recruiting a Diverse Workforce
- * Involvement in Co-Op/Inroads Programs
- * Diversity Training
- * Mentoring Program with predominantly minority schools

4) What was the implementation strategy/approach used for your Diversity Practices?

- * Assessing where the organization is and the organization's needs
- * Defining the meaning of diversity to the organization
- * Identifying barriers to efforts
- * Developing a comprehensive strategy
- * Developing a marketing and cost strategy both internal and external

5) How do you measure the success of your organization's diversity practices?

- * Conduct employee/attitude surveys
- * Conduct employee/management focus groups
- * Track the number of EEO charges/grievances
- * Monitor employee turnover rate and reason for leaving

* Conduct exit interviews (especially minority employees)

6) What advice would you give to your colleagues about starting a Diversity Initiative?

   * Have top management support and commitment
   * Clearly define what diversity means within your organization
   * Ask employees what they want/need
   * Incorporate diversity goals into management's performance appraisals
   * Educate management and employees on what diversity is to the organization

7) What makes you most proud of your Diversity Practices?

   * Our program is designed to help our people understand what diversity is. They hear the word 'diversity' and have no idea how it affects them every day. We continue to receive high evaluation ratings at the end of each workshop.

Roberta took this information to the rest of her Diversity Initiative Committee, and it was of considerable assistance to them.

NETLIVING NOTES:

* Netliving with members of other cultures will help your understanding of diversity. I've learned to treat people as they want to be treated.
* Netliving through volunteer organizations helps you to grow culturally. I've learned by stretching my world to include new experiences opens up new cultural exposure.

* Netliving with colleagues improves your understanding of diversity. I've learned sharing experiences with peers helps all aspects of my life.

CHAPTER EIGHTEEN

TO UNDERSTAND THE LANGUAGES OF LOVE

"Let my love like sunlight surround you, yet give you illumined freedom."

Rabindranath Tagore (1861-1941)

Richard sat in his soft leather recliner and sipped his morning coffee while he read the daily newspaper. It is the end of the century, and all is not well in America. Society is split, racially and economically, into two increasingly isolated groups: the have's and the have-nots. As new technology emerges, many fear its influence and the loss of privacy.

Reformers pledge to change the "spoils system" of politics, he read. They charge that government is falling into the hands of vulgarians and corrupt elected officials. One popular definition of "politic" comes from two Latin words -- *poly* which means *many* and *tic* which is a *blood sucker*. "Conspicuous consumption" by the wealthy comes under fire, as materialism and greed run rampant. And Congress, as usual, gets the worst of it. "Congress is as disorganized, stupid and childlike as ever," charges a critic. Our very culture appears to be on the brink of destruction. The end of twentieth century civilization in a nutshell?

By the end of the nineteenth century, Mark Twain had dubbed that era of excess and crushing poverty as "The Gilded Age," citing the veneer of glitter that covered its decaying core. It all sounds familiar, thought Richard. The details of the 1890's may be different from today's, but the fundamental anxieties are remarkably similar. The fears about technology in 1890 centered on the telephone, invented just 14 years earlier. Richard read that when Louis Brandeis and fellow attorney, Samuel Warren, wrote their famous "Right to Privacy" in 1890 they fretted about the telephone, "Numerous mechanical devices threaten to make good the prediction that what is whispered in the closet shall be proclaimed from the housetops." Now, a hundred years later, the bogeyman threatening to proclaim our secrets from the housetops-- not to mention our valuable credit card numbers -- is called "the Internet."

There are many who believe that the automobile, the television and the Internet have contributed to the growing coarseness of our culture.

The common denominator shared by these inventions is their ability to isolate individuals or help them effectively communicate -- especially the automobile and the Internet. This condition is compounded in the short-on-daylight days of winter.

This raises a natural question: Is the current alarm over the decline of civility more of the same? The fear is genuine, but is the decline? Hoping to find the answer, conservatives and liberals alike have formed new commissions to study the decline of civility. Members of Congress, known for their occasional lapses in decorum (e.g. The Impeachment Hearings) went on a retreat last spring to learn how to get along. And 89% of Americans believe, according to a recent poll, that the problem of incivility is a serious one.

In his recent book, Arthur Herman, of George Mason University, argues that the evidence does not support our national malaise. Western cultural ideals and institutions enjoy more prestige now than ever before, the world over. Not only that, but we live in a time of such unparalleled freedom and material abundance, our ancestors would be positively dazzled.

Yet despite this positive evidence, Richard read that there remains a "prevailing gloom about the fate of American society." This deep, unshakable pessimism can be traced back more than 200 years to Edward Gibbon's massive chronicle of the death of a great civilization, published -- coincidentally -- in 1776, just as the future American empire was being born out of dreams and conflict.

Gibbon's book *The Decline and Fall of the Roman Empire* became highly respected and widely read throughout the world. Gibbon's conception of the Roman empire as doomed to self-destruction from within because of its successes and excesses had a profound impact on the modern historical imagination. The idea that modern civilization might one day disappear, despite its material and political endowments, Richard thought, was haunting this and future generations.

Judith Rodin, president of the University of Pennsylvania, formed a commission to study "the nuclear explosion of incivility." She agrees that decline is a perennial social worry, and that incivility is nothing new. What has changed is our ability to access: "Without mass media, nobody knew except the few people who heard the speech or whatever. And I think that the accessibility of all of these instances to the general public has just raised the ante so much."

So, Richard thought, Americans can dismiss the nagging feeling that their culture is decaying or they can do something about it.

"I think what is most distressing about this is that people recognize in their own behavior things that they really don't like and find upsetting and objectionable," Professor Rodin says. "But they feel sort of carried along in this wave of incivility," she concluded.

Ralph Waldo Emerson said, "Life is not so short but that there is always time enough for courtesy."

There is love in courtesy. It says I care about other's feelings, that I wish to contribute to their comfort and well-being.

Above all, courtesy is treating people as I would like to be treated, Richard thought. I can be courteous, even when I am angry or hurt, without compromising what I believe is right. Courtesy has nothing to do with right or wrong, it has everything to do with self-respect, which is the well spring of respect for others.

Richard also felt strongly about the concept that it is important to show courtesy to children as well as to adults. Courtesy is taught at home by parents who act courteously toward their children. There are many benefits in showing children courtesy, beginning with the self-esteem it assists in fostering.

Richard thought about how much netliving principles had helped him to act with courtesy toward himself and others. This behavior contributed toward his feeling good about himself, and enabled him to share the benefits with others. He especially enjoyed sharing this feeling of well-being with his sister, Roberta. They spent many hours discussing how they could be more civil to each other and to the friends, family and associates they come in contact with on a daily basis.

What American society needs now is what Johann Wolfgang von Goethe wrote many years ago: "There is a courtesy of the heart. It is akin to love. Out of it arises the purest courtesy in the outward behavior."

Courtesy of the heart may seem detached; it does not interfere with another's decisions or give advice or need approval. It neither plays games nor passes judgment; it does not accept guilt or make others feel guilty. Courtesy of the heart, Richard found, does not distinguish between the president and the busboy, can never feel snobbish or superior, and is able to learn from everything and everyone. Courtesy of the heart welcomes new ideas and people, feels joy instead of fear, sees with fresh eyes and appreciates rather than criticizes what it sees. He prayed to be blessed with the ability to show "courtesy of the heart" to all.

Richard believed that God is the source of all love. God has said that when two or more gather in My name there is love. Many songs and poems have been written on the subject and many a love story has been told. But what is "love" -- really? It is a difficult word to define. It is a feeling, and it is different at various stages of life, (from the adolescents' puppy love" to the mature "golden wedding anniversary" variety).

At a family reunion that Richard attended a few years ago, a preacher made an attempt to explain love. He spoke about the five languages of love:

1) Words -- "Written, spoken and sung. In this category, prayer is the greatest example of love. Though I may feel frustrated or angry, I reach out in an attempt to give up my will for God's, my pride for humility. Prayer is

recognizing healthy qualities as well as defects. Prayer is the power ready to be tapped by an open mind. Prayer turns my thoughts toward instead of against, me showing me that I want to change. I pray to see those defects and self-deceptions that keep me from being spiritually whole. I pray for the clarity to see honestly, to be rid of illusions. A loving heart makes its own prayer, and prayer makes for a loving heart."

2) Touching - hugs, handshakes, holding, and patting. "What is so great about hugs? There's no such thing as a bad hug -- there are only good ones and great ones. They're not fattening and they don't cause cancer or cavities. They're all natural, with no preservatives, artificial ingredients, or pesticide residue. They're cholesterol-free, naturally sweet. And they're a completely renewable natural resource. They don't require batteries, tune-ups, or x-rays. They're nontaxable, fully returnable, and energy efficient. They're safe in all kinds of weather; in fact, they're especially good for cold or rainy days. And they're exceptionally effective in treating problems such as bad dreams or the Monday blahs. Moral: Never wait until tomorrow to hug someone you could hug today."

3) Service - Doing for others without any thought of repayment. "Service is defined as 'an act of helpful activity; the rendering of assistance or aid.' Some colleges and universities require a certain number of hours of community service in order to graduate. One of the joys of community service, a student commented, 'Is the interesting people you encounter.' The late Mother Teresa indicated in her book, *Blessed Are You,* 'The fruit of love is service.' The characteristic that she and the late Princess Diana had in common was the loving service both gave to the least of their brethren." (The first principle of netliving is giving without expectation of reward).

4) Quality Time - One-on-one sharing of one's self with another human being. "Generally women are much better at this than men. Sharing what is happening in your life and the lives of others forms the essence of girls' and women's friendships. 'Troubles talk' is just one aspect of the ongoing intimate conversation that can be called 'gossip.' Women friends and relatives keep the conversational mechanisms in working order by talking about small things as well as the large ones. 'For most women, getting together, expressing their feelings, and describing what is happening in their lives is at the heart of their friendships. Having someone to tell your secrets to means you are not alone in this world.' 'For most men, talk is primarily a means to preserve independence, negotiate and maintain status in a hierarchical social order. This is done by exhibiting knowledge and skill, and by holding center stage through verbal performance such as storytelling, joking, or imparting information. From childhood, men learn to use conversation as a way to get and keep attention. So they are more comfortable speaking in larger groups made up of people they know less well -- in the broadest sense, 'public speaking.' "In effect, we end up with many situations where men and women have divergent sensitivities. Thus, 'sensitivity training' judges men by women's standards, trying to get them to talk more like women; while 'assertiveness training' judges women by men's standards and tries to get them to talk more like men"

5) Gifts - Flowers, jewelry, perfume, candy, after shave, ties, cards, etc. "Some people are much better at picking gifts for other people than are others."

Richard felt his sister Roberta had a talent for picking just the right gift for anyone whether they were two or eighty-two. He also felt his wife's dominant way of showing love was through service.

The most interesting point made by the preacher he felt was this: "Most people instinctively want to receive love through the language they use most often to express their own love."

"Love is expressed in action by caring, doing, remembering, and listening. Love is being strong enough to put one's own problems aside to help another. Love cannot flourish in the presence of obsession; there is no room for it. Romantic songs notwithstanding, it takes emotional maturity to be capable of showing consistent, enduring love."

After reflecting on all this reading and exploring his own thoughts, Richard was grateful that he had established a network of friends and family to netlive with him on a daily basis. He felt strongly that what the world needs right now is more love and less incivility.

A reading from the founder of Overeaters Anonymous sums it up quite well: "I put my hand in yours. . .and together we can do what we could never do alone! No longer is there a sense of hopelessness, no longer must we each depend upon our own unsteady willpower. We are all together now, reaching out our hands for power and strength greater than ours, and as we join hands, we find love and understanding beyond our wildest dreams."

NETLIVING NOTES:

* Netliving will make you aware of the incivility of our culture. I've learned it is a lot easier to react than it is to think.
* Netliving will open our minds to giving service to those in need. I've learned that in order to have a balanced life I must reach out to others.
* Netliving will help teach us to love one another. I've learned there is love in courtesy.

CHAPTER NINETEEN

TO OBTAIN PEACE OF MIND

"A simple Path through Life -- The fruit of Silence is Prayer. The fruit of Prayer is Faith. The fruit of Faith is Love. The fruit of Love is Service. The fruit of Service is Peace."

Mother Teresa (1910-1997)

A foreign exchange student from Calcutta, India had become friends with Roberta when her parents sponsored the student while he attended a local university. During lengthy discussions about the differences between America and India, he mentioned meeting Mother Teresa when he was a young man in Calcutta. This revelation led to many long conversations about the saintly woman who was one of Roberta's all-time heroines.

Mother Teresa, the frail, Nobel Peace Prize-winning nun who ministered to the poor, sick and dying and came to embody charity and goodness for countless millions, had actually sat and talked with this young Indian man. Roberta took advantage of the opportunity to ask endless questions.

Mother Teresa, Roberta learned, was born Agnes Bojaxhiu on either August 26 or 27, 1910, to Albanian parents in Skopje, about 200 miles South of Belgrade. Blessed with abundant churches and mosques, the city is today the capital of Macedonia. Accounts have differed as to the profession of Mother Teresa's father. An authorized biography of her, published in Britain in 1992, stated he was a building contractor. While a schoolgirl, she belonged to a Catholic lay women's group. At its meetings, letters were read from Balkan Jesuits who had traveled as missionaries to Bengal, in eastern India.

The more Roberta learned about Mother Teresa, the more questions she asked. The young Indian went on to say that at the age of twelve Mother Teresa first felt the desire to become a nun.

At eighteen she decided to do so and got in touch with the Sisters of Loreto, an Irish Catholic order with missions in Bengal. She joined the order in Rathfarnham, a suburb of Dublin, in 1928. After English lessons there, she spent more than a year in Darjeeling, north of Calcutta, where the Order ran a girls' school.

The young nun became a teacher of geography, history and catechism at St. Mary's High School, on the grounds of the Entally Convent outside Calcutta. It was while riding on a train September 10, 1946, that she received her "call within a call." She left her school and learned nursing skills from other nuns. Then she began her good works among Calcutta's poor, feeling uncertainties at first but also experiencing happiness as she set about meeting peoples' needs. "I knew where I belonged," she recalled, "but I did not know how to get there."

In 1950, Roberta was told, Mother Teresa established the Order of the Missionaries of Charity, becoming its Superior General. She went on to organize diverse and far-flung programs for the impoverished, eventually reaching more than 90 countries. The number of sisters in her religious order (only 62 in 1957), grew enormously. By the time Mother Teresa won the Nobel Prize, her order had attracted 1,800 nuns and 120,000 lay workers. She operated more than 80 centers in India and more than 100 -- largely children's homes -- in other parts of the world. The order's patients included 53,000 lepers. Roberta was amazed at this accomplishment since she had trouble visiting a maternity ward in a local hospital.

As Roberta and the Indian student continued to chat, he went on to explain that over the years her work had expanded. She set up mobile health clinics, centers for the malnourished, rehabilitation hospices for lepers, homes for alcoholics and drug addicts, and shelters for the homeless. Her centers in the United States included the Gift of Love Hospice for 15 men with AIDS in Manhattan's Greenwich Village.

Yet, the nun who was widely considered a living saint also had her critics. Roberta's friend pointed out their objections to her staunch opposition to abortion, in keeping with Vatican doctrine, (in fact when she was in New York City to address the

United Nations she would not have her picture taken with President Clinton because of his position on abortion) and to some of the company she kept. "Mother Teresa is a religious imperialist who believes that Hinduism and Islamic teachings are wrong and Catholicism is right," charged Australian-born feminist Germaine Greer, who met Mother Teresa in the first-class cabin of an airliner in 1972. "She is not ministering to the poor of Calcutta for their sake, but for the sake of her Catholic God."

Catholics and admirers from other faiths (including Roberta's Hindu friend) were outraged by such talk, but the target characteristically was unruffled. "All I can do is pray for them," was Mother Teresa's customary reply to her critics. Her only goal in life, she liked to say, was simply to do "something beautiful for God." To her original religious vows of poverty, chastity and obedience, Mother Teresa added a fourth vow: "wholehearted and free service to the poor," a vow that is unique to the Missionaries of Charity.

In 1952, the fledgling order opened the Hirmal Hriday (Immaculate Heart) Home for Dying Destitute in Calcutta. Those first years were hard, and Mother Teresa had no shortage of opponents and detractors. Some Hindus demanded that authorities stop her activities because they suspected that she was forcing large numbers of destitute Indians -- Hindus, in the main -- to convert to Christianity in exchange for food and shelter. Others wondered what one woman with a small band of helpers -- the order numbered just 27 sisters in 1953 -- could do to alleviate the suffering of the hungry, homeless and dying in the poverty-ravaged metropolis that Rudyard Kipling vividly dubbed "the city of dreadful night."

"We ourselves feel that what we are doing is just a drop in the ocean," Mother Teresa acknowledged. "But if that drop was not in the ocean, I think the ocean will be less because of that missing drop." Roberta's friend indicated that one of the secrets to Mother Teresa's success was her strong network of supporters. In some cases, she won over the officials who initially opposed her.

Some Hindu hard-liners remained suspicious of her work and intentions until the end. But the vast majority of Indians considered her an inspiration and a national treasure. "To meet her is to feel utterly humble, to sense the power of tenderness, the strength of love," the late Indian Prime Minister Indira Gandhi wrote.

"I have said often, and I am sure of it, that the greatest destroyer of peace in the world today is abortion," Mother Teresa said in a message to the 1994 U.N. Conference on Population in Cairo, Egypt, thereby renewing controversial remarks she had made in her Nobel acceptance speech. "If a mother can kill her own child, what is there to stop you and me from killing each other? The only one who has the right to take life is the one who has created it." Roberta's friend noted that not many things raised her blood pressure, but the subject of abortion was one of them.

Both inside and outside the Roman Catholic Church, the tiny octogenarian was a larger-than-life symbol of faith, kindness and hope in a confusing, materialistic and violence-marred age. "My life is dedicated to God, and I have never interfered in politics, of which I know nothing," she said in 1995. "See human beings as God's children, with the right to live in love, peace and harmony." Former U.N. secretary-general Javier Perez de Cueller once said of Mother Teresa, "She is the United Nations. She is peace in this world." As Roberta listened to many stories of Mother Teresa, she was reminded of a reading from the first letter of Paul to the Cornithians, (Chapter 12 versus 12 through 31 *Saint Joseph Edition The New American Bible)* "THE BODY is one and has many members, but all the members, many though they are, are one body; and so it is with Christ.

"It was in one Spirit that all of us, whether Jew or Greek, slave or free, were baptized into one body. All of us have been given to drink of the one Spirit. Now the body is not one member, it is many. If the foot should say, 'Because I am not a hand I do not belong to the body,' would it then no longer belong to the body? If the ear should say, 'Because I am not an eye I do not belong to the body,' would it then no longer belong to the body? If the body were all eye, what would happen to our hearing? If it were all ear, what would happen to our smelling? As it is, God has set each member of the body in the place he wanted it to be. If all the members were alike, where would the body be? There are, indeed, many different members, but one body. The eye cannot say to the hand, 'I do not need you,' any more than the head can say to the feet, 'I do not need you.'

Even those members of the body which seem less important are in fact indispensable. We honor the members we consider less honorable by clothing them with greater care, thus bestowing on the less presentable a propriety which the more presentable already have. God has so constructed the body as to give greater honor to the lowly members, that there may be no dissension in the body, but that all the members may be concerned for one another. If one members suffers, all the members suffer with it; if one member is honored, all the members share its joy.

"You, then, are the body of Christ. Every one of you is a member of it. Furthermore, God has set up in the church first apostles, second prophets, third teachers, then miracle workers, healers, assistants, administrators, and those who speak in tongues. Are all apostles? Are all prophets? Are all teachers? Do all work miracles or have the gift of healing? do all speak in tongues, all have the gift of interpretation of tongues? This is the Word of the Lord."

In 1982, Mother Teresa went to Beirut to help victims of Lebanon's civil war. When Ethiopia plunged into a killer famine, she placed a telephone call to the Reagan administration, which soon afterward dispatched $64 million in urgently needed aid. These were members of the body of Christ.

When acquired immune deficiency syndrome surfaced as a global menace to health, she opened hospices to allow AIDS patients to die with dignity. These were members of the body of Christ.

Mother Teresa was awarded the Nobel Peace Prize in 1979 for her charitable work with beggars, orphans, lepers and other afflicted human beings. These were members of the body of Christ.

"The hallmark of her work has been respect for the individual's worth and dignity," John Sannes, chairman of the Norwegian Nobel Committee, said at the December 10, 1979, ceremony in Oslo, Norway. "The loneliest and the most wretched, the dying destitute, the abandoned lepers have been received by her and her sisters with warm compassion devoid of condescension, based on this reverence for Christ in man." these were members of the body of Christ.

Attired in the $1 white habit she wore throughout her ministry, Mother Teresa appeared before the white-tie gathering to accept the prize "in the name of the poor." These were members of the body of Christ.

On September 5, 1997, in her 87th year, Mother Teresa, the diminutive nun whose very name became synonymous with caring for the world's poorest souls, passed away. She was mourned worldwide. Her death means "there is less love in the world, less compassion, and less light," said President Jacques Chirac of France. "She leaves us a strong message which has no borders and which goes beyond faith: helping, listening and solidarity."

K.R. Narayanan, the president of India, said her death represents "an immense loss" to millions of poor Indians who were touched by her charity and her embrace of the culture of the Asian subcontinent. "Such a one as her rarely walks upon the earth," he said.

The Vatican noted that Pope John Paul II was quickly informed of the death and immediately prayed for her. He celebrated Mass the following day at Castel Gandolfo, his summer residence outside of Rome. "Her death touched his heart very deeply" because of his appreciation for her commitment to the poor, reported the Rev. Ciro Benedettini, a Vatican spokesman. Cardinal John O'Connor of New York was visibly upset as he spoke to reporters in New Jersey, where he attended a service ordaining a new bishop. "The world loses a woman who walked this world," O'Connor said, pausing to regain his composure before continuing, "... in as holy a fashion as any woman I've ever known.

Coretta Scott King, widow of the slain civil rights leader Dr. Martin Luther King, said in Atlanta, "Our world has lost the most celebrated saint of our times. This courageous woman gave hope to millions, and showed us the power of caring and human kindness."

As the world's most well-known ethnic Albanian, Mother Teresa drew immediate tribute from the leaders of troubled Albania, Europe's poorest country, which was trying to recover from a chaotic revolt that brought virtual anarchy in the spring of 1997.

Roberta recalled the words of Ralph Waldo Emerson: "Nothing can bring you peace but yourself." Mother Teresa was part of a world that searches for possessions and prestige as if they are the keys to happiness. Owning certain luxuries is recognized as "living well."

But is it, really? Living well is an internal condition, not an external one. Here was a woman who wore a $1 nun's habit and lived with the poorest of the poor, but she had the inner peace that comes from giving service to others.

We cannot will ourselves to have peace of mind, but we can re-examine our priorities, Roberta thought. Are we putting enough time and effort into activities that nurture our spirit? Are we learning that what our lives need is the elimination of clutter and excess, which take up time, space and energy. If we think we need something, we ask ourselves, What will it add to the quality of our lives? The true source of serenity, of good feelings, is not getting what we want, but wanting what we've got.

NETLIVING NOTES:

* Netliving will increase your knowledge of great people. I've learned many people "Talk the talk," but only the great ones, "Walk the walk."

* Netliving helps one to understand what is important in life. I've learned my joy will show from what I do and say in going about the everyday business of living.
* Netliving teaches us that peace of mind is an inside job. I've learned to judge by deeds and not just words.

CHAPTER TWENTY

PRE-RETIREMENT PLANNING

"If one advances confidently in the direction of his dreams, and endeavors to live the life which he has imagined, he will meet with a success unexpected in common hours."

Henry David Thoreau (1817-1862)

A Task force on Aging was established by the Vice President of Human Resources at Richard's firm, and he was named chairman. The group consisted of the following: Plant Manager, Human Resource Administrator, Materials Manager, Regional Sales Manager, Engineering Manager, Organization Development Consultant and the Plant Human Resource Manager (Richard).

The primary mission of the group: "To study the effects of aging on the firm's current and future work force." Specifically, they were charged with "reviewing current policies and practices so that they will favorably reflect current government regulations and the firm's philosophy."

Prior to the first working session, Richard distributed current literature on the then-mandatory retirement age and other possible areas of concern. In the first working session, Richard used a brainstorming approach to help the group develop the following list of concerns and issues:

The Plant Manager had been with the company slightly over a year and had been a plant manager in two other frozen food plants prior to his arrival at his present position. He had worked as a human resource manager for seven years prior to his recent plant management experience, and brought a balanced production/people approach to the group.

He brought up the following points:

* Help design jobs better; assess for medical issues that are job related.
* Define job to be sure person can do the whole job.
* Reduce number of employees by automating heavy lifting jobs.
* Concerns with the viability of the Social Security System.

The Human Resource Administrator had been with the firm for over fifteen years and had been involved in human resource work for the entire period. She had been involved in human resource policy decisions and had a good grasp of the company's history in dealing with employees and human resource matters. Her issues were:

* What impact this new law (changing mandatory retirement age) will have on benefits; fringe benefit increases; know how much will be allowed with government provided guidelines.
* Inflation may keep people from retiring and has a definite impact on fringe benefits.
* Be sure retirement benefits can assure desirability of retiring.

The Materials Manager had been with the company less than a year, but he represented a critical portion of the firm's operations and had been involved in the same area of work with another food company. He listed the following areas of concern:

* Better performance appraisal program: start applying performance appraisal early in an employee's career so it does not suggest age discrimination.
* Family members still dependent for longer period of time -- beyond the death of the employee. How should pension plans be handled? What about survivor benefits?
* Safety in the work place -- concerned about Workers' Compensation.

The Regional Sales Manager had been with the company over twenty years and had advanced through the plant power structure. He had been hired as a young man out of college and had been with the firm ever since. He was familiar with the plant workers as well as the field sales force. His issues were:

* View retirement as dignified experience -- relating to the age limit.
* How do we announce company's response to "new"mandatory age law?
* The pluses and minuses of this age group by positions to help evaluate all factors; can the group accept the results?
* What should the company policy be on work after reaching firm's retirement age?

The Engineering Manager brought an analytical and practical approach to the task force that helped to keep it on an even keel. Although he had only been with the company for a year and a half at the time, he had many years of prior experience in another frozen food plant. He expressed the following concerns:

* Redesign equipment for more comfort, i.e., space and height of production line so operators can sit at the work place.
* Capitalize on what an older person has to offer the firm.
* Education level is now higher for employees; not as willing to work on lower level jobs.

The Organization Development Consultant had been affiliated with the company for a considerable length of time and brought a broad field of knowledge to the group. A Ph.D. psychologist, he had been working in the business world for many years. He pointed to some areas of opportunity:

* Create jobs for older workers; increasing problems with hourly workers after reaching age sixty five: standing

eight hours a day, being in a refrigerated atmosphere for eight hours a day.
* Keep young hard-chargers in the company to continue youthful excitement.
* Stay current; review task force's progress.
* Consider providing work opportunities for employees who are un-promotable but still productive (plateau employees).

The final task force member was Richard who at the time had fifteen years experience in his field and had worked for several other companies. He was currently studying for his MBA with a specialty in the area of human resource management. Most of his experience had been as a human resource generalist in a manufacturing setting and he had a good overall grasp of his function. He voiced several concerns as follows:

* Develop a process to talk to people planning to retire.
* Pre-retirement counseling two to three years prior to retirement (age 55?).
* Second Careers; what age to start such counseling (62?55?).
* Review company's demographics.
* Obtain more data on workers age (65-75).
* Profile Index.

As a follow-up to this meeting, Richard contacted the engineering department and asked them to keep the older worker in mind when designing new equipment and new production lines. He used an example that the Engineering Manager had used in the task force meeting. Many jobs in the plant could be done from stools so older workers with weak feet and legs could still continue to perform.

In April, the task force met again to discuss and evaluate a current situation involving a female employee who had been with the firm for approximately twenty years. She was competent as a machine operator, completely dependable, known and liked by everyone. In fact, she was an "institution" at the plant.

When she had reached age sixty-five, the supposed mandatory retirement age at the plant, she was given the usual retirement party and bid a happy retirement. A few weeks later Richard's predecessor received a call from her daughter, who was upset. The family felt that the former employee was practically dying of a broken heart from missing her machine and the plant people so much. Being people oriented, the company bent the rule and reunited the worker with her fellow employees and her beloved machine.

However, problems quickly developed. This older employee had become accident prone. She had fallen twice and broken bones both times. There were also a few near misses with the machine she loved so much. She carried her tool box so she could make minor repairs, but she was not as quick as she used to be.

Using this dedicated older worker as a concrete example, the task force came up with the following ideas and suggestions:

a. Move her to a less dangerous production job, based on her safety record.
b. Offer her a non-production job off the production floor away from most of the safety hazards.
c. Plan some sort of phase-out program from now until she reached age seventy-one.
d. Reduce her hours of work and use her as a consultant to help orient new employees while at the same time combining with pre-retirement counseling.
f. Make sure that all of her fellow workers know that she is being treated properly.
g. Make sure her daughters understand what the company is trying to accomplish.

Richard reviewed all of these ideas and came up with a final proposal. He did some netliving with other human resource managers in his geographic area and did some benchmarking with them. The plan required her supervisor to meet with her and review the safety record. He would express the firm's concern for her safety and suggested the alternative of having her work in the linen room until she retired on her seventy-first birthday. If this arrangement was not acceptable, she would be allowed to work on her beloved machine a few more months until her final day on the job.

As the plan was implemented, the results were not what was expected. She was cooperative and appreciative and recognized the company had bent the rules when she was sixty-five. She agreed to retire in one month. She stayed with "her" machine until the end.

The company hosted a gala retirement party that her daughters attended. She went out with a blaze of glory. Richard followed up with her from time to time. She had begun another career as a baby-sitter at a local nursery school. At the company family picnic, she did not miss dancing one of the polkas.

Considering this experience, Richard decided it was important to find out if similar cases existed and how they felt about retirement. He developed an age profile of the work force and conducted a survey to determine how the employees felt about retiring at age sixty-five versus seventy.

Another important outcome of this case was gaining approval to develop a pre-retirement planning program. Since Richard had shown such interest, he was given the assignment of developing the new program.

As with many other new programs, Richard began by netliving with human resource managers in his geographic area. He visited several of them to determine what type of pre-retirement programs they had instituted and what they covered.

Also as was his custom, he had a long telephone discussion with his sister, Roberta who was part of the same profession and had many contacts in her network that Richard could netlive with to obtain benchmark data on the subject.

In discussing the subjects that should be covered in a pre-retirement planning program, Richard began to develop a list to use as an outline for his firm's program. All agreed there was a need for a session on "Retirement Concepts" dealing with the "Transitional Passage Into Retirement." There was a need to review the old and new definitions of retirement. "Attitude Changes and Adjustments" was discussed and listed as important. "Overcoming the myths of Aging" and exploring life planning concepts was done, making sure the three L's were taken into account -- Labor, Learning and Leisure. (See Chapter 8, Figure 8-1, Old Life Planning Model)

The importance of "Planning for Retirement" was an item mentioned often in these telephone conversations. Learning about transition management issues and a session on developing and identifying ones own retirement satisfaction issues was suggested. A definition of *RETIREMENT* was given: an event, a process, and a social role that requires ongoing planning of the key elements of my life, based on a renewed awareness of my unique interests, needs, values and skills. This planning must result in written goals, timetables and action steps to be taken.

Retirement is a relatively new concept that is still changing. In the past, retirement was seen as an ending. The primary focus was on leisure and the mistaken idea that retirees are too "old" to be active. Some even felt that it was a process of slow withdrawal from life and there was a strong penalty for growing old. Some felt that the end of an organizational career meant an end to all productive work.

In the nineties, Richard found that retirement is viewed as a new beginning. The focus is on learning, labor, leisure and self-oriented values. There is a strong feeling of freedom from restraints imposed by others. The new thinking regards retirement as only withdrawing from work orientation as a primary activity. Retirement is thought of as a reward due for many years of hard work and sacrifice.

What has caused this change in attitude toward retirement? There are many factors that have come into play. For example, Richard learned that in 1920 the life expectancy of a male in the United States was fifty-four years. In 1997 the life expectancy of a male is seventy-six years. This increased longevity is due to great medical advances and the gradual change to more healthy lifestyles.

Richard discovered in his netliving that more liberal company pensions are available to employees as well as 401k programs provided by the federal government under the internal revenue code. These factors have enhanced the trend toward early retirement. Also, early retirement buy-out packages have been a boon to early retirement.

In addition, an increase in second careers and other employment options have made a big change in the concept of retirement. The volatile climate in the business community had increased the amount of outsourcing, which has created more post-retirement employment in the form of consulting contracts.

In the original concept retirement was considered a linear progression. One phase was completed before the next phase began. For example, an individual completed the learning phase of life before entering the labor phase, and the leisure phase did not begin until the labor portion was completed (See Chapter 8, Figure 8-1 , Old Life Planning Model).

Richard then became aware of the new life planning model that has three phases -- early years, middle years and later years. However, he found each phase contains a combination of the three L's; Labor, Learning and Leisure. In the early years, the emphasis is on learning, but here is also an element of labor and leisure. In the middle years the emphasis is on labor, but there is an element of learning and leisure. The later years focus on leisure, but some work and some learning are included, which add an overall balance to life's journey (See Chapter 8, Figure 8-2, New Life Planning Model)

In the first session of his program the subject of overcoming the myths of aging was covered with some effort. Richard realized the Madison Avenue advertisers have done a strong disservice to the older person by painting a false picture of them. Many people have been led to believe that the majority of older people (past age sixty-five) are senile. Many believe that all five senses tend to decline in old age. The general public feels most old people have no interest in, or capacity for, sexual relations. There is a strong feeling that lung capacity tends to decline in old age, and that the majority of old people feel miserable most of the time. Most believe that at least one-tenth of the aged are living in long-stay institutions. In fact, Richard found that all the above statements are false.

In further study of the myths of aging, Richard found it a common belief that most older people are set in their ways, unable to change and almost incapable of learning new things. He found these statements to be untrue.

In the second session of the program, Richard had an articulate representative from the Social Security Administration come in and explain the social security system and Medicare. It was felt by Richard and the people with whom he netlived, the most important subject of the entire program would revolve around money -- how much money will I receive if I want to retire early? If I continue to work part-time, how much will they (Social Security and Medicare) take out of my pay? Also, how will this effect my Social Security Benefits? What are the "Notch" years (born 1916-1921) and how will that affect me? Can widows retire at age sixty? If I retire at age sixty-two, who will pay for my medical coverage?

Fortunately all of these questions were answered and the group was ready for the next session that dealt also with money. Two benefit representatives from the firm spoke in detail on the retirement plan, the 401k plan and all the related company benefits at retirement. They went through all the requirements an employee must meet to qualify. For example, if you are retiring at the age of sixty-five or later, you must have been hired prior to your sixtieth birthday. In addition, you must have completed five years of active service as a full-time employee prior to your sixty-fifth birthday.

If retiring early, you must be at least age fifty-five and have completed ten years of service. At least five of these years must have been as a full-time employee. In order to be covered by company benefit plans, you must have been covered by company benefit plans prior to retirement.

The explanation of the 401k plan was straightforward and most employees were familiar with its terms since they were interactive with if from its inception. The benefits at retirement covered life insurance and health care coverage for the retiree and dependents.

In the fourth session, Richard had decided to invite a financial planner to discuss the important subjects of Finances,

Estate Planning, Taxes and Budgeting. This was a heavy subject load but caught the interest of all the participants. The feeling was that to have a comfortable retirement, these four subjects needed to be addressed by the potential retirees with some knowledgeable professionals.

In the fifth session, the services of one of the company's attorneys were used by Richard to explain the legal aspects of retiring and gave each participant the information needed to protect their legal rights. An official from the Retired Seniors Volunteer Program (RSVP) came to speak to the group regarding leisure time activities/community resources and the volunteer opportunities and second careers.

The RSVP official pointed out that what retirees want in a second career was found in a 1988 *Modern Maturity Magazine* poll of over four thousand retirees that produced the following results:

* Very few primarily motivated by money, prestige, or status.
* New criteria: zest, adventure, new people, or meeting a "perceived need."
* Many constructed second careers from the most enjoyable part of their first careers.
* Many sought the challenges of entirely different job or new settings.
* Leisure goals -- e.g., travel -- often combined with employment goals.
* "Demotion" acceptable due to greater concern with lifestyle/reduced stress.
* Missing the work itself a factor with involuntarily retired; for others, missing the social context was a primary motivation.

Health concerns, nutrition and deciding where to live were the topics of the sixth session. Richard had lined up a professor of health and physical education and a real estate expert to facilitate these topics.

Understanding the key elements of nutrition, exercise and stress management were the main areas of the first part of the session. The speaker laid out a positive prevention health and fitness plan for the participants to adopt. He also pointed out several NUTRITION ACTION TIPS:

* Proper diet will help prevent heart attacks and combat stress/illness.
* Reduce fat -- the average American gets 45% of his/her calories from fat; this should be lowered to 30%.
* Increase fiber -- fiber protects against cancer of the colon and prevents heart problems.
* Eat more fresh vegetables -- research shows a lower risk of cancer.
* Reduce sodium intake -- excessive sodium consumption can aggravate high blood pressure.

He also listed the many benefits for exercising regularly:

* Strengthens heart and lungs
* Increases flexibility
* Curbs appetite
* Relieves stress and anxiety
* Helps you sleep better
* Keeps you mentally alert
* Improves your appearance
* Creates a sense of well-being

When Richard introduced the real estate expert, she reviewed the key housing facts/issues. She pointed out that less than five percent of people sixty-five or older relocate. Of the five percent who relocated, twenty-five percent had downscaled. Nearly half of those over sixty-five lived in one of eight states: California, Florida, Illinois, Michigan, New York, Ohio, Pennsylvania or Texas.

She pointed out there are many residential alternatives; present home, smaller single family home, rental apartment, condominium or in cooperative, duplex residence, retirement apartment, retirement community, campus plan or multi-facility, retirement hotel or club, living with adult children or other relatives or a mobile home.

Currently the living arrangements for persons sixty-five years of age and older is as follows: Men -- seventy-five percent live with spouse, eighteen percent live with other relatives, and seven percent live alone or with non-relatives. Women -- forty-three percent live with spouse, eighteen percent live with other relatives, and thirty-nine percent live alone or with non-relatives.

Richard had arranged to bring in a group of recent retirees in the seventh and wrap-up session to relate their experience as retirees to the group. Fun and humor made this session memorable. A big graduation cake and ice cream ended the sessions with some fanfare.

Ten years later, when downsizing came to the company, many of the graduates of the pre-retirement training program came to Richard to thank him for preparing them to accept early retirement buy-outs.

NETLIVING NOTES:

* Netliving will help you plan your retirement. I've learned in planning, "Two heads are better than one."
* Netliving will enhance the quality of your golden years. I've learned by building a safety network of family and friends my life is happier, healthier and more rewarding.
* Netliving will insure your health and well-being in retirement. I've learned that sharing with honesty, openmindedness and willingness improves my journey through life.

CHAPTER TWENTY ONE

THE HEALING POWER OF LAUGHTER

"A cheerful heart is a good medicine, but a downcast spirit dries up the bones."

Proverb 17:22 (Revised Standard Version)

John Dolan, Roberta's father, was a great story teller (*Seanachie* in the Gaelic) and most of his stories had humor permeated throughout them. He told family sagas that had been passed down to him from his father and his grandfather before him.

Roberta admired this in her father and attempted to emulate him in this regard but it did not come naturally at first. She always considered herself an *optimist* for she habitually saw or anticipated the best. She almost always saw "the glass half full, rather than half empty."

In fact Roberta tried hard to see the humor in life. She found in her professional life as well as her social life that humor is a "social lubricant." She would try hard to remember a good, clean joke and tell it to all of her friends and fellow workers. It made her feel good to get a laugh or even a smile.

When Roberta was a youngster she and her brother, Richard would fight over who would be first to read the *comics* in their local newspaper. She was a big fan of *Blondie* and *Peanuts,* while Richard loved *Beetle Bailey* and *Garfield.*

This daily routine gave them a constant infusion of humor that helped them cope with the small stresses they were faced with such as homework assignments and upcoming tests. As Roberta grew older and went off to college she lost the habit of reading the "funnies" as her brother and she referred to them.

While attending a Human Resource Conference she found herself in a conference room where the subject of the session was "Basic Humor First Aid and Instructions." The presenters were Kenneth J. Kovach and Gary Bunch. Their basic premise was: "Why we should be serious about humor in life and 'how to' use humor effectively in decision-making, problem-solving, and inter-personal relationships."

They mentioned a book written by Norman Cousins that Roberta had heard of called *Anatomy of An Illness* that was first published in 1976 where he told his discovery that 10 minutes of solid belly laughter would give him two hours of pain-free sleep. He was suffering from cancer and since his illness involved severe inflammation of the spine and joints, making it painful even for him to turn over in bed, laughter became a significant feature of his treatment.

At the time, little was known about the ability of the human brain to produce secretions with morphine-like molecules -- endorphins and enkephalins. Looking back he realized that laughter probably played a part in activating release of endorphins.

In writing about his experience, he was careful to point out that he didn't regard the use of laughter as a substitute for traditional medical care. Cousins also emphasized that in order to recover he brought a full range of positive emotions into play -- love, hope, faith, will to live, festivity, purpose, and determination" (Quote from Norman Cousins in *Psychology Today/October 1989)*

Roberta learned that humor could enhance communication by being an asset to establish a climate of trust and candor. She knew from her own experience that this was especially true when it came to dealing with teenagers. Humor can support the understanding and retention of information and can assist in establishing rapport. Many times she recalled remembering an important point in a speech when the speaker told a funny story.

In a group dynamics situation, humor can be used as a means of reducing problems to a more manageable size in a creative problem-solving opportunity. Humor can support more creative and flexible approaches to solutions. Roberta found that research on creativity supports the idea that humor and play are helpful to the process. She also became aware that humor can help conflict management in a group dynamics situation. The relief of laughter can give people a chance to rethink their approaches and to see alternatives that may not have been obvious before. She found it is almost impossible to laugh heartily and to be angry at the same time. The use of humor in a conflict situation is a potentially "high-risk/high-payoff" intervention.

Guidelines for the effective use of humor were presented to Roberta and the rest of her class. The students were asked to start with themselves. They must be able to take their work seriously but themselves lightly. They must observe what is going on around them. They must think of humor as being of two kinds, public and private. Roberta and her fellow classmates were urged to use humor as a support for competence rather than as a means of masking a lack of competence. It was suggested that they use humor with sensitivity and care so that it is likely to be appreciated.

There was a strong parallel between tapping into her creative potential, Roberta felt, and thinking positive and seeing the humor in work and other family related situations. To see herself as having challenges, rather than problems. Her knowledge of netliving promoted collaboration, cooperation, and cross-fertilization of ideas (seeking out different people with different perspectives). She then defined her challenges clearly.

During the afternoon session of the *Humor* seminar, Roberta learned about "comic vision" where a person re-frames reality. This can be accomplished by spending five minutes each day making believe you're Alan Funt with "Candid Camera" or are looking through the eyes of a six-year-old child at all situations.

The seminar leaders also suggested she develop her own "Weekly Humor Journal," where she would document 'how' and 'where' humor came into her life, as well as 'how' and 'where' you gave the gift of humor. It was also suggested that she develop her own "Humor First Aid Kit." This was comprised of a three-ring binder where collected materials were organized for quick use.

The first thing that came to mind for Roberta was her friend in Atlanta who e-mails her a different joke at least three times a week. She in turn passes these gems of humor along to many of her family, friends and acquaintances who are on her e-mail address book.

Roberta and her fellow classmates were reminded to Practice, Practice, Practice. They were told to LAUGH AT YOURSELF, LAUGH WITH OTHERS and take every opportunity to practice the above.

Excited at what she had learned at the seminar on humor, Roberta wanted to put it into practice immediately. As soon as she arrived home she called her brother to netlive with him and share what she had learned that day.

She gave him a *Reader's Digest* version of the subject and immediately launched into a story about a camping trip:

> Sherlock Holmes and Doctor Watson went on a camping trip. After a good meal and a bottle of wine they lay down for the night, and went to sleep. Some hours later, Holmes awoke and nudged his faithful friend. "Watson, look up at the sky and tell me what you see." Watson replied, "I see millions of stars." "What does that tell you?", asked Holmes. Watson pondered for a minute and responded:
>
> "Astronomically, it tells me that there are millions of galaxies and potentially billions of planets."
>
> "Astrologically, I observe Saturn as Leo."
>
> "Horologically, I deduce that the time is approximately a quarter past three."
>
> "Theologically, I can see that God is all-powerful and that we are small and insignificant."
>
> "Meteorologically, I suspect that we will have a beautiful day tomorrow."
>
> "What does it tell you?"
>
> Holmes was silent for a minute, then said, "Watson you YAHOO, some bastard stole our tent."

Richard roared with laughter over the phone and of course had a little story to tell his sister not be outdone:

Four gray-haired ladies were returning home from a card party along a rural route and a highway patrolman happened to notice they were traveling at a rather low rate of speed. He turned on his radar and clocked them at twenty-two miles per hour. He followed them for a mile or so and decided to pull them over. As he approached the car the driver said, "Officer, officer. Why did you stop us?"

"We were not speeding," she continued.

As the trouper asked her for her driver's license and owner's card he noticed that all three of the passengers were WHITE AS GHOSTS. He said to the driver, "Ma'am, the reason I pulled you over is that you were going 22 mph in a 55 mph zone. She said indignantly, "Officer I was just following that sign over there, look it says '22'."

The trouper immediately realized what had happened and said, "Ma-am that is the route sign -- this is route 22." Then he returned her driver's license and owner's card and said, "Okay ma-am, You can go now, but I am curious about one thing." "Why are the other ladies so white and scared looking?" he questioned. With a sheepish expression she replied, "We just came off route 128."

It was Roberta's turn to give a big belly laugh and this pleased Richard. She was so happy that she was eager to try some of this new knowledge on other friends and relations.

Both she and Richard had the same thought at practically the some moment -- they made a vow they were returning to reading the comics on a daily basis. The also discussed a mission they were presently attending. It was a five consecutive night program that was led by a Franciscan Friar by the name of Father Scott. Scott was a native Pittsburgher with a strong Western Pennsylvanian accent and had a tremendous sense of humor. He used it effectively in his talks.

Many of his points were made with a funny story. He quoted Victor Hugo as saying, "laughter is the sun that drives winter from the human face." Father Scott told the story about confession as follows:

> When Mrs. O'Flaherty went into the confessional, she noticed an unfamiliar face behind the shutter.
> "You're not our regular priest," she said. "Who are you?" "I'm the furniture polisher, ma'am,"the man said. "Well, where is Father Devine?" She asked. "I couldn't tell you, but if he has heard any of the stories I've been listening to, he's gone for the police."

Father Scott echoed many of the points on humor that Roberta had heard in the seminar she had just completed. He talked about Norman Cousins and how he had helped heal himself by renting "Abbot and Costello" movies along with the "The Three Stooges." He would sit for hours and watch gleefully with loud belly laughs at the antics of these funny people on the screen.

"Humor, like religion, has a way of cutting a pompous strutter down to size... Humor is a moral banana skin dedicated to the discomfiture of all who take themselves too solemnly."Father Scott quoted Halford Luccock.

Some of the topics Father Scott covered in the five nights were: Sunday -"A Christian Response to Stress," Monday - "Celebrating Marriage and Family Life," Tuesday - "The Art of Forgiveness," Wednesday - "Finding True Happiness" and Thursday - "Give Hope a Chance." Throughout all five of his sermons, Father Scott peppered the theme "The Healing Power of Humor."

In the middle of a serious discussion about honesty he would interject a little funny story:

> A young man was called into his boss' office. "Joe,"the boss said, "Do you believe in life after death?"
> "Yes, sir, " Joe replied. " I do too," the boss said,"An hour after you left to attend your grandmother's funeral, she came to see you."

Roberta finished the mission feeling recharged. The humor seminar and the funny stories she heard in the five days of the mission by Father Scott had given her a degree of hope that was not there before.

The other byproduct of her recent experiences was she felt much more creative. Roberta felt with this new insight she would enjoy and use humor as much as possible (there is a direct relationship between "ha ha" and aha")

While reading the local newspaper she noticed an article entitled, *Humor is a vital tool in the workplace.* Here at the tail end of the stress-filled, hard-knock 90s, more companies are praising the benefits of humor in the workplace. Especially since they've found that those employees who laugh, last. In employment interviews, major corporations like Ben & Jerry's Ice Cream and Southwest Airlines even incorporate questions about how candidates use humor to cope with stressful situations. 'Sometimes when people come into an interview, they think they have to be serious and not smile,' said Edward Leigh, president of Edward Leigh Enterprises Inc., who travels the U.S. giving presentations on humor in the workplace. 'Then the interviewer thinks there're stiff, so they're not sure the person will fit in or be able to deal with stress.' That search for a sense of humor works both ways, too, since there's nothing wrong with asking an interviewer what the company does for fun, such as annual outings, sports teams, dress-up days for professional sports days (Super Bowl), etc. People already employed should apply humor as a way to relieve the pressures of their job responsibilities. Leigh suggests always including a fun activity on the omnipresent 'to do' list: taking five minutes to read the funnies or play with a slinky or another fun prop on their desk. More and more smart employers are encouraging such levity breaks, too, since studies show that not only does humor relate directly to creativity, but there is also a definite link between humor and health."

With this new perspective on humor Roberta expanded her exchange of jokes and funny stories with some of her long time college friends on the Internet. In one of her training classes on the job she decided to use the following story she obtained from the Internet to make a point about assumptions:

> A Marine colonel on his way home from work at the Pentagon came to a dead halt in traffic and thought to himself. "Wow, this traffic seems worse than usual. Nothing's even moving." He noticed a police officer walking back and forth between the line of cars, so he rolled down his window and asks: "Excuse me, Officer, what's the hold up?" The officer replied:
>
> "The President is just so depressed about his Impeachment Trial he has stopped his motorcade in the middle of the Beltway and he's threatening to douse himself in gasoline and set himself on fire. He says his family hates him and he doesn't have the $ 35 million he owes his lawyers. I'm walking round taking up a collection for him. "Oh really?" said the Colonel, "How much have you collected so far?" The officer replied: "So far only about three hundred gallons but I've got a lot of folks still siphoning."

Roberta was shocked at the mixed reaction she received from her class. Most of the participants took it good humordly and laughed. Others were indignant and felt it was inappropriate for a business setting. One of the lessons about humor she just learned the hard way is that it must be appropriate for the audience and obviously this was not the current case.

Even with this momentary setback, Roberta felt this new appreciation of humor would help to keep her energy level high. She also resolved to take the "I" out of "idea" (deal with the issues, not the personalities) piggybacking on the ideas of others. In other words "Escape from the center of the universe." And take myself lightly and my work (or problem) seriously.

NETLIVING NOTES:

* Netliving can help develop your humor skills. I've learned there is something pure, cleansing and healing about laughing at myself.
* Netliving helps eliminate negative thinking. I've learned when I receive a lemon to turn it into lemonade.
* Netliving humor improves our health. I've learned that joy, lightheartedness and laughter are "internal jogging."

CHAPTER TWENTY TWO

ON THE INTERNET

"Where there is an open mind, there will always be a frontier."

Charles F. Kettering

Although Richard had been hired by IBM off the college campus, he had never become computer friendly while in their employ. He had taken a few courses on programming but it did not interest him in the least.

As the technology improved and personal computers became more friendly, he began to consider buying one for home use and since his company was becoming more aggressive in the area of computer use he felt knowing more about them wouldn't hurt. The children had also been vocal about the need for one in the home so they could play computer games and learn the use of these modern communication devices.

Richard had always been the type of person to jump into the water and then decide to learn how to swim. He was the one who bought the toy for the children and had it assembled before he discovered there were instructions for putting it together -- step by step.

Since this purchase involved a substantial amount of capital, Richard decided to netlive among his "Webhead" friends and associates who were familiar with "cyberspace" terminology and current trends in hardware and software. His two main resources were his number two son, Peter and his daughter, Maureen, both of whom had graduated with honors from Purdue University's Computer Technology program and were currently working as consultants for "big six" consulting firms.

Since, Peter (who is four years older) had more experience with PCs and was willing to contribute half the cost of the system , he became the primary resource. They laid out a "game plan" to accomplish this mission. First, both Peter and Richard would netlive with their friends who owned computers to determine which was the most popular at the present time. Richard had a loyalty to IBM (due to his prior employment there and his present stock ownership), but Peter insisted they leave emotions from the plan since this was a business decision. And "Dad," he said sounding like an echo, "You have always insisted that 'business is business."

Ironically both father and son owned stock in IBM since Richard had been an employee and had stock options and had set up portfolios for each of his three children.

Netliving many of his friends and associates he concluded that Gateway 2000 was the best deal so he called the 800 number and ordered the latest PC model available. This machine had all the bells and whistles a webhead could wish for in their wildest dreams. It had speakers with music and sounds that were much clearer than the family's stereo system. It had a pentium processor and a built-in modem with fax as an option.

When the boxes arrived with the new system, Richard and Peter were like kids at Christmas time. As he pulled components out of the box, Peter would give a hoop and holler. He assembled the pieces and parts in record time for he wanted to get on the cyber superhighway.

Peter had already saved a free disc from America On Line and before the sun had set he was on-line sending e-mails to all his friends and associates. He also installed a group of computer games which he and his friends enjoyed immensely.

Richard was pleased to see his son so happy, but he was a bit terrified of this new investment. He was fearful that he could mess the whole system by pushing the wrong buttons. Peter assured him that these newer personal computers were built with safeguards that prevent the type of horror story that had been told to Richard by many of the friends of his generation.

In the back of Richard's mind he was planning for retirement. He felt if his current company had any mergers with other companies he would opt to seriously consider a buy-out and set up his own human resource consulting business right in his condominium.

Having the PC and laser printer were a good start in the right direction. He would need to purchase a plain paper fax machine that could be used as a copy machine for business purposes. Then he ordered an additional phone line that could be dedicated to the computer and eventually used in the consulting business. There were also now on the market digital answering machines that would either take a voice message or a fax depending on the electronic signal it received.

One of Richard's friends gave him a book called, *300 Incredible Things To Do On The Internet* by Ken Leebow (1997;VIP Publishing, Marietta, Ga.). His friend recommended it as the best selection of Web sites he'd ever seen. He gave a list of destinations from Leebow's wide range of "fun and useful" selections:

FUN AND EASY INTERNET (www.thebee.com/bweb/brand/htm) are perfect for people who received their first computer and need help in plain language to race over the Internet.

LOOK SMART (www.looksmart.com) has more than enough resources, including dozens of destinations for career chasers and job shoppers.

RESOURCES TO BURN (www.beaucouo.com/engbig.html) aptly describes Beaucoup!, a page that helps you find almost anything: search engines, reviewed sites, media, geographical targets, software, literature, language, educational databases, music, arts, graphics, science, nature, technology and more.

DICTIONARIES ONLINE (www.onelook.com) is the perfect fast finder for spelling or use of a term on your cover letters and resumes. Topics vary from business terms and statistics to technology and telephony.

MY VIRTUAL REFERENCE DESK (www.refdesk.com) draws on the world's largest library, the Internet, to answer questions that could wear even the most energetic reference librarian. The thesaurus and quotations link page will blow your socks off.

INSPIRATIONAL ACHIEVERS (www.achievement.org) are profiled in this site of people who have been successful in business, art, entertainment, sports and other areas of society. Profiles include their advice for achievement hopefuls.

PEOPLE FINDER (www.westminster.ca/cdnlook.htm) is a great place to find someone's e-mail address, telephone number and postal mailing address.

TELPHONE TRACKING (www.infospace.com) is a compendium for yellow and white pages, city guides, investing databases, on-line shopping guides, and just for fun, horoscopes and daily lottery results.

E-MAIL CORRESPONDENTS (www.liszt.com) may be what you need to e-mail somebody who has the data you need to jump jobs or career fields. This site's 84,792 mailing lists is organized by category. The official jobs category is thin, but you may be able to scoot around and find just what you need.

The e-mail section was the area of the Internet that Richard latched onto immediately. He obtained the e-mail address of his high school friends, his college buddies, business associates and far-flung family members. The family member the greatest distance away was a cousin located in the United Kingdom who had happened to be visiting Richard's aunt in Pennsylvania where they met and discussed the family tree and cyberspace among other subjects.

This cousin, Tommy, had many of the same interests as Richard so they spent quite a bit of time together. They exchanged e-mail addresses and have been corresponding on a regular basis ever since. They found the mode of communication effective and quite inexpensive.

When a job opportunity came up which required high technical skills Richard was quick to access the internet to pursue candidates that might be webheads. He would us his America On-line Member Directory to determine suitability of candidates. This service would list a profile by member name, location (by city, state and country) birth date, sex, computer literacy, hobbies and occupation.

An article in the local paper caught Richard's eye -- *Free Seminar Reveals "How to" Make Money on the INTERNET!* The ad went on to state "The Internet can be the link between a great idea, product or service, and marketing it successfully." This convinced Richard that he should attend. What did he have to lose except a block of time and some car mileage.

The following Saturday morning found him in a large meeting room at the nearby Holiday Inn with a group of would-be entrepreneurs. The facilitator began the program by stating, "We in America are entering a new frontier." He continued, "The Information Superhighway is going to be more exciting than the Industrial Revolution." Richard thought to himself this guy is smooth. He obviously has been well trained and has done this session many times. He had it down pat.

The gifted speaker went on to say, "It is time to get INTERNET SMART." He continued by saying, "The Web rush is on. It's everywhere, and it's putting the whole world at the fingertips of ordinary people turned Cyber-preneurs, people of all ages and from all walks of life." Richard could relate to this based on his experience with his cousin in the UK. The facilitator went on with great energy, "In less than two years, the Internet has become a force of such magnitude that it is considered by many to be the fastest growing phenomenon in the world today."

Armed with the knowledge he had acquired at the seminar, Richard was anxious to try it and see the results. He was currently attempting to fill a high profile information systems position that would require national recruiting.

Knowing his boss was a hard-sell on new ideas, Richard laid out a detailed proposal on placing the ad for this technical opening on the Internet to explore the new frontier. He went in with both guns loaded with information and he was amazed that his boss bought the idea without many questions.

What they agreed to was to use their existing ad agency to place the ad in cyberspace rather than jumping immediately into establishing their own website. They were a company of evolution and not revolution.

One of the questions Richard's boss had for him was "What is the Internet? Since he had just attended the free seminar, Richard had the answer on the tip of his tongue. He said eagerly, "The Internet is a cooperatively run, globally distributed collection of computer networks that exchange information via a common set of rules for exchanging data. It started about 20 years ago as a government funded project that would allow communications in the event of a nationwide nuclear attack.

The Internet was primarily used by the government and educational institutions until about five years ago. E-mail was the first real business application. However, within the past 36 months, business and electronic retailing have discovered that the Internet is the most powerful communications system the world has ever seen. Since that time, it has been referred to as the Information Super Highway."

His next question was "What is the difference between the Internet and the World Wide Web?" Again Richard was ready, "The Web (World Wide Web) is the most exciting and revolutionary part of the Internet. The Web is a collection of millions of computers on the Internet that contain information that has been put in a single format agreed to by everyone - a format called HTML (hypertext markup language). By combining multimedia - sound, graphics, animation, and more - with incredible ease of use and connectivity among its many different parts, the Web has become the most powerful tool in cyberspace.

The Web is becoming a part of everyone's life, from students doing research to professionals sharing information to kids learning and being entertained. But, the most explosive area for the World Wide Web is in commerce - doing business. More importantly, each month tens of thousands of shoppers turn to the Web for selection, price, and ease of use. The growth of this medium has been explosive!"

With this new information Richard's boss felt comfortable in having him use it to recruit high tech computer professionals.

The ad agency was excited to hear they were interested in placing an ad on the Internet. They worked with Richard to put it in a format that would catch the eye of the job-seeking IS (Information Systems) professional. Part of the deal was the ad would run for thirty days and would be placed in a high traffic area of Look Smart (which has dozens of destinations for career chasers and job shoppers).

Fortunately, Richard had also tapped into his netliving network and had run ads in the traditional newspapers. After a month of anxious waiting he contacted the ad agency to see if they had received any resumes from the Internet and their response was they had received zero.

This was a great disappointment to them and a greater one to Richard. He went to see his boss with hat in hand and explained that it was fortunate they had not spent more than the few thousand dollars they had spent on the ad. The good news was that he had hired a strong candidate that was acquired through netliving.

Richard felt it would be a while before his company was ready to develop their own Website because of the poor showing of the ad, but he still felt strongly that the Internet was the way to plan for the future.

He read an article in the local paper: "Webheads will be major players in the 2000 campaign." The article read, "So how much did the Internet affect the 1998 mid-term elections? Some, but nowhere near as much as the PC Webheads say it will alter the voting in 2000. The invisible but not-yet-invincible PC network that eliminates geography in politics, as in everything else, helped re-elect a U.S. senator by a handful of votes, enabled a professional wrestler to become governor by running under the old media's radar screen, and sparked a grassroots rebellion that dampened the impeachment campaign when Congress saw the numbers. But the Internet does not yet pack the political wallop of television. As older heads recall, radio did not kill off newspapers, TV didn't kill radio, and the Internet, while an impressively dynamic new collection medium, probably will not obliterate the old mediums. But it will instead layer over them."

By the time the next election rolls around in 2000, Richard vowed to himself that he would be much more familiar with the use of the Internet and use it to stay abreast of the political scene.

Overall he felt that the internet was a great netliving tool and he especially liked e-mail for he used it every day to keep in touch with both distant and not so distant friends and relatives. He enjoyed most of all the jokes and funny stories his college friend from Atlanta furnished him on a regular basis.

NETLIVING NOTES:

* Netliving can assist you in purchasing computers. I've learned to ask many questions of the people surrounding me who have the answers.
* Netliving on the Internet can be fun and profitable. I've learned that the computer is not as fragile as I once thought.
* Netliving using e-mail is an inexpensive mode of long distance communication. I've learned as a former "ham" radio operator that e-mail is an updated version of communication.

CHAPTER TWENTY THREE

TO WALL OFF HISTORY

"You can do anything if you have enthusiasm . . Enthusiasm is at the bottom of all progress. With it, there is accomplishment. Without it, there are only alibis."

Henry Ford (1863-1947)

A decaying stone wall built in 1904 along a state route and bordering the village in which Roberta and her family lived was "between a rock and a hard place." She found the reason for this position was technically the wall was owned by the state because it was situated on state land. It seems that years ago when the state department of transportation wanted to add another lane to the state route it took the land on which the wall was built by "eminent domain." This gave the village the "out" they were looking for, so the village manager and his board of trustees threw up their hands and said they would not be able to repair the wall with taxpayer's money since the wall was located on state property. The spokesperson for the state says, "the department of transportation does not have enough money to finance the nearly $60,000 that the restoration would cost."

This is the point where Roberta entered the scene. She was a member of the board of managers for her sub-division that happened to be adjacent to the historic wall. The first question she had for anyone who would listen was, "Why do Americans spend thousands of dollars each year to travel to Europe to look at old buildings and structures but when it comes to the United States of America all they want to do is knock down old structures and replace them with shinny new ones." She continued to ask, "What was wrong with this picture?" The more she discussed this issue with her neighbors the more she became convinced that the only way to solve the problem of repairing this beautiful work of art and craftsmanship was through a grass-roots effort.

Roberta found two other residents who shared her deep concern regarding saving this historic landmark. Dick was a retired carpenter who had a well-rounded knowledge of construction and Jake was a retired police chief who had many contacts in the community.

Jake was a member of the village board of trustees and had been asked by the village manager to do some research on the wall and report back to him his findings. Jake found that the wall was built in 1904 with flat creek bed rocks. In his further search he found the wall was built by local mason William Burke Thompson, who also constructed cemetery vaults and decorated a bridge at the local zoo. Thompson who lived nearby died in the early 1940s.

The dimensions of the wall, Roberta found, were 881 feet long, three feet high and a foot wide. "The mortar between the stones is raised, like the icing on the edge of a cake," she said.

After discussing the wall with Dick and Jake, Roberta thought of an idea that might help to save the wall from the wrecking ball. Her idea was simple but workable. The idea was to form a committee made up of village residents and approach the 1200 plus neighbors for donations to repair the wall. One of the incentives for those who gave at least one hundred dollars would be to have their name on a bronze plaque that would be mounted in a visible place. Both Dick and Jake liked the idea. Jake had already talked to eleven potential mason repair people. He indicated the verbal, non-binding quotes ran from $5,000 to $60,000. Roberta said immediately, "Now I know where the figure of $60 k that appeared in the local paper came from." "The reporter picked the highest number for effect." she continued.

Dick, Jake and Roberta decided to throw out the highest and lowest bid and average the remainder to come up with a working amount of $15,000. This they felt was a reachable amount but it wouldn't be easy.

"In addition to financing problems," Jake said, "locating a stone mason who is trained to restore field stone is becoming increasingly difficult." "I've talked to a few old timers, but stone masons just don't do this kind of work anymore." he said. "It's really an art form. At one point in history, masons did what they called 'beading,' similar to decorating a cake. No one has the patience or the equipment for this technique anymore. All the old timers are in their 80's, retired or gone." Jake concluded.

Through his research Jake had found that ten years earlier an auto had run into the wall and the insurance company paid to have it repaired. "Unfortunately the person they hired to fix it was not a qualified stone mason and the repair did not hold up." he said.

The small committee decided they needed to expand and recruit more members to complete this formidable mission. Each of the three were to recruit three more members that would give them a workable group of a dozen.

In August of 1997 the first full-scale committee meeting was held at Roberta's condo. The first order of business was to establish leadership. It was decided that Jake, Dick and Roberta would be co-chairs. This gave them representation from three different geographical areas of the village. That way they could communicate the progress of the fund raising to their neighbors.

The committee liked the idea of having a bronze plaque with the names of those who contributed at least $100. They felt this would be a great incentive for contributions.

The committee decided they needed an attractive flyer to publicize the campaign. Fortunately an accomplished artist and computer graphics expert was on the committee and she volunteered to come up with a few versions of a publicity piece for the committees' approval.

In addition it was decided that an escrow account would be opened at the local bank so that all funds would be deposited in it to earn interest and have checks to pay for necessary materials and services. The three co-chairs were authorized to sign checks and handle the account.

The other issue that was decided at this first meeting was that the committee needed to keep the village manager informed of its activities out of courtesy. It was further decided that

Roberta would make that contact since Jake did not get along well with him and Dick was not one of his favorite people.

Roberta called the village manager when she got home and he was cool to the idea of a grass-roots approach to solving the wall repair problem. He said, "Why not wait for the local politicians to come up with the money?" We pay taxes for this and it is on state land so hold off and let the state pay for it." he continued. She indicated to him that a representative of the state indicated there were no funds to repair the wall and if it became too unsightly they would just knock it down with a wrecking ball. He went on to reiterate what he had told Jake earlier, "I feel strongly that we cannot use village revenues to repair the wall since it is on state land." Roberta told him that she and her committee were going to proceed with the grass-roots fund raising but she would concede to him that letters would be written to the state asking again for funds to repair the wall.

At this point Roberta had no idea what a battle this committee was going to have with the village administration. All the way up and down the organization from the receptionist on the front desk to the village manager, any request or inquiry the committee-for saving-the-wall brought up, received heavy critique and whenever possible denial.

In the second save-the-wall committee meeting the flyers were reviewed and all three of them were accepted because they had turned out so well. It was felt by the group that a variety of forms would be helpful. The graphic artist designed a logo for the Save-the-wall's official stationary that was attractive.

The co-chairs filled out donor slips and wrote personal checks in the amount of $100 to kick off the fund raising drive and the balance of the committee were urged to do the same since it is difficult to solicit others for donations when you have not shown a good example yourself.

At the second committee meeting it was decided to have Jake contact the local newspapers to see if they would run a human interest story about saving the wall. The committee also wanted to place an article in the local village newsletter that was distributed to all residents each month. Since Roberta had a computer and was a decent writer this task was assigned to her.

There was a brief discussion regarding the adversity the committee was receiving from the administration and methods of coping with it were reviewed. Many of the members had some pieces of information to confirm the feelings of the co-chairs.

The members were encouraged by the first month's efforts. The Save-the-wall committee had raised nearly two thousand dollars. The question of picking stone masons for repairing the wall came up so it was decided that Jake would arrange all the quotes and the co-chairs would interview all bidders who met the specs which had been reduced to writing.

As the fall wore on the funds began to drop off. At this point the amount collected was approaching 66% of the goal and the campaign was showing some signs of losing momentum. Then Roberta came up with another idea to promote interest in the campaign. She and her husband owned a summer camp in a nearby state and she felt they could raffle off a weeks vacation for the following summer. The proceeds would be sent to the Save-the-wall account. When she mentioned this idea to her spouse there was a long silence. He was not as warm to the idea as she was but after a lengthy discussion agreed to go along with the concept.

When the idea was discussed with the rest of the committee there were some concerns expressed by some of the members that it was taking a big risk on the part of Roberta and her husband. She blew it off by saying they would place a legal statement on the back of the raffle tickets that would hold the user liable for any damage to the property.

Once they overcame that hurdle there were other questions that had to be addressed. It was revealed that in this state you could only conduct a raffle if you were a not-for-profit organization. When the co-chairs looked into what it would take to establish non-profit status it was a red tape nightmare. So they decided to be sponsored by some non-profit organization. This was not an easy task. Dick approached the local historical society but they turned the idea down cold. Jake talked to a couple of organizations and received the same response. Their logic was they did not want to be involved with other than their own fund raising.

Finally Roberta came up with a group known as Friends of the Village. They were a non-profit organization and were hurting for members. Their charter was to go around the village and help to keep it beautiful by planting flowers and other plantings. They asked the Save-the-Wall committee to have some members attend their next meeting and the topic would be raised and voted on by the members present. A couple of the Save-the-wall committee also belonged to FOV so they were willing to go to the meeting. The result was the motion to have the Friends of the Village sponsor the Save-the-wall campaign was passed by a large margin.

The Save-the-wall committee expressed their gratitude and made a commitment to help FOV with their rummage sale in the fall. Now Roberta went to the bank to give them the magic non-profit number so all of the interest that had been earned was now tax free. The flyers for the raffle were made by the local artist and the second phase of the campaign to save the historic wall had been launched.

Roberta held a meeting at her place to assemble all the raffle tickets. It was decided by the committee that it would be better to have a numbered raffle ticket so there would be no question as to the authenticity of the winner's ticket. This called for gluing a ticket stub to the top and bottom of each flyer. This seemed like an easy task but proved to be time-consuming and messy.

When it was completed each of the twelve committee members took 100 raffle tickets and began netliving with their family, neighbors, co-workers and acquaintances. The price was $5 each or three for $10. The value of the weeks vacation was estimated at $500. This raffle gave a second wind to the committee and helped push the drive over the top eventually.

Jake, Dick and Roberta took turns sitting at a table in the local shopping mall selling tickets every sunny afternoon. One day they approached a local artist (who ran a framing shop) to take a chance or give a donation, he opted to donate a beautiful colored painting of a rainbow trout that was nicely framed. This caused a discussion with the committee; some wanted to add the painting as a second prize of the vacation drawing and others felt it should have its own separate drawing. The idea of the separate drawing won out and the tickets for it sold well.

The raffles were held in the village hall and the winners were notified of their good fortune. The overall proceeds from the raffle were approximately $2500 and stimulated people who had not heard of the Save-the-Wall campaign to give large and small donations. Even some young children gave their candy money for this worthy cause. One lady (who did not live in the area but passed the wall on her way to and from work every day for twenty years) gave at nice check towards its repair. By June 2, 1998 the goal of $15,000 had been reached.

The final phase of the campaign was helped by the repair activity taking place on the wall starting the first week in May. The co-chairs had interviewed at least a dozen groups of masons in the month of December, to no avail. These candidates were either not qualified or were too expensive.

By chance Roberta ran into an old friend while attending lunch with a retired fellow worker for Christmas. This chance meeting with the gentleman from Ireland who owned a stone cutting business proved to be the answer to the save-the-walls committee's repair needs. He had been a good friend of Roberta's landlord for her first two years of college. After passing the seasons greetings and finding out how all their mutual friends were doing, Roberta asked him if he was still in the stone business. He indicated he was and the business was booming.

She explained to him her project and her needs and he said he had just the lads who could do the job for them. He made an appointment with Roberta to come and look at the wall. She checked the date with her co-chairs and they met the red-faced Irishman at the wall. He looked it over and said his two masons could do a fine job of this wall repair. The only problem was they were retired and living in Florida. He quickly added, "However, they will be coming back north in late April and he would put them in touch with us." He also gave them a good tip about the bronze plaque they were planning to mount on the wall.

"Don't do it," he said. "I have made lots of money from firms who place bronze plaques outside," he continued. "They get stolen and melted down for other things," he concluded. We had heard this from some of the other masons we had interviewed but since Roberta knew him so well they were convinced.

Finally the two Irishmen know as the "stonemen" came back from Florida and contacted Roberta. She had them come out to see the wall and they were convincing regarding their ability to handle the job. When it came to cost the co-chairs could not believe what they were hearing. They were asking less than half what the others who were not as qualified wanted. They volunteered they only wanted enough money to keep them in spending money and they would only be working six hours a day and three days a week. This was great with the committee because they still had some donations to obtain and had all summer to have the wall repaired.

As soon as they began repairing the wall there was another surge in donations. People passing by would honk their horns and encourage them to keep up the good work. One of the co-chairs would walk over to see them every day they were on the job. It was the answer to many prayers. They did a wonderful job.

The next challenge the committee faced was getting the plaque prepared and mounted. The thought was that a mock-up would be made on paper and enclosed in the monthly newsletter of the village. The village manager had other ideas. He was on his high horse and said, "He was not doing any advertising in his newsletter for the committee." He would not let it appear. Finally after many discussions he relented but would not allow a note to accompany the mock-up to explain that if anyone saw a mistake to let the committee know. It finally went out alone and the village office received many phone calls from puzzled neighbors.

The other hassle the committee picked up on was the village manager was not in favor of us mounting the bronze plaque on the inside wall of the village hall. The committee had a meeting and it was decided the only way to beat the system was to circulate a petition signed by a good number of the citizens of the village since the village was owned by the tax payers. The committee went to work diligently and had well over three hundred signatures on the petition that stated the plaque should be hung on the inner wall of the village hall.

This really upset the manager. He was angry and brought in the village attorney to invent a legal reason why they should not place the bronze plaque on the wall of the hall. He went through a great deal of trouble and taxpayers money to make sure that plaque was not installed in the hall.

At the next monthly village town hall meeting all the committee to Save-the-Wall attended and the village board of trustees were to vote on the issue. The village manager saved the plaque issue until last on the agenda and in an authoritarian manner talked down the idea of placing a plaque in the building. They took a secret vote and there were only two votes in favor of placing the plaque on the wall in the village hall.

Jake was so angry he made a lunge for the village manager and members of the committee had to restrain him to keep him from grabbing the manager by the throat. Jake's wife was also enraged and gave the village manager a piece of her mind. What made the manager so angry was that some of the village trustees had signed the petition. On the other hand what made Jake, his wife and the Save-the-Wall committee so angry was these trustees had signed their names to the petition and then in secret reneged under pressure from the iron-fisted dictator of a village manager.

The Save-the-Wall committee met to decide what to do about the plaque and again Roberta had a contingency plan that was well received by the rest of the committee. She proposed that they resubmit quotes to the plaque makers and ask for bids on aluminum versus bronze plaques. Her research indicated there is evidence that aluminum plaques are not targets of theft at all. With the plaque made of aluminum (which is about 40% cheaper) there would be less fear of it being stolen if it were mounted on the stone column at the end of the historic stone wall.

At this meeting one of the committee members suggested that one of the neighbors who owned a plaque making company be included on the bid list. It sounded like a good idea to the co-chairs. He might even give them a break on the price they thought.

Roberta commenced to send out new requests for bids for the aluminum plaque. One of the bidders called back and said he could do the job at a reasonable price but his company could only do it in capital letters. After consulting with the other two chairs she told the bidder they would have to be upper and lower case letters for there were some people on the list who had both capital and small letters in their surnames.

Then a quote came in from their neighbor stating a price that they knew was out of line for it was as high as previous quotes for a bronze plaque. Roberta was disappointed since this person was a neighbor. When he called her about the quote she told him she had received it but there was no sample with it and they were waiting for the other bids to come in. He indicated he would send a sample soon. In the meantime another bidder came in with a price that was where they felt it should be. It was $1800 versus the $2800 the neighbor was charging. The co-chairs decided that Jake should contact this neighbor in writing to let him know that the committee had chosen another vendor. This decision was made since Jake was not as close to this neighbor as Dick and Robert.

The committee went ahead and visited the lowest bidder's facility to take a close look at samples of his work. After viewing those samples they wrote him a check for half the cost of the project. The balance would be paid at the completion of the plaque.

Meanwhile the neighbor who had submitted the high quote wrote a nasty note to Roberta telling her she had given him a verbal okay to proceed with the plaque and the subcontractor had begun the work. Roberta wrote a return letter quoting the terms of the contract that called for everything to be in writing and that there had been no verbal approval given from her or any member of the committee.

Once again it underlined the point that it can be a hazard to do business with family, friends or neighbors. The plaque was being cast and ready for mounting on the stone pillar at the east end of the historic stone wall that spring. The committee had submitted the necessary paperwork to have the historical society declare this an official historic site. This historic status will insure that any future plans to widen the state route have to take place on the other side of the road.

Jake found an article entitled, *Preservationists build support for old walls,* written by Tracy Watson and appearing in the February 2, 1999 edition of USA TODAY, that seems to indicate their Save-the-Wall committee was on the national cutting edge. The article indicated that states from New England to California have begun wall-protection programs. "Some states , such as Vermont, merely discourage landowners from knocking down walls. Others require those who knock down highly visible walls to rebuild them. California is trying to get some of its walls on the National Register of Historic Places. Stone wall building in the USA began when settlement did. Farmers in New England had to clear out the stones before planting crops. They also used walls to keep cattle in and wild animals out, and used the plentiful local stone, pieced together without mortar, to build their fences. "

Roberta continued to read, "Later, some walls were built around the grand horse farms of Virginia and Kentucky and along the highways in Oregon and California. . . No one seems to know how many stone walls are in the country, let alone how fast they're disappearing. But Mitch Wagener, a professor at the University of Connecticut, estimates his state alone has at least 20,000 miles of wall. And an inventory in the county that's home to Lexington, Ky., estimates that between 1967 and 1990, the county lost 25% of the walls gracing its horse and family farms.

People hate seeing nearby walls torn down, and state and local officials don't like seeing history destroyed. 'To keep Vermont looking traditional, stone walls are an important element,' say Curtis Johnson of Vermont's Division Of Historic Preservation. . .

Dick pointed to the paragraph that stated, "Other wall programs:

- In Rhode Island, if a road is widened, the stone wall alongside will be rebuilt. Most of the walls are 'balance walls' without mortar.
- In Fayette County, old stone walls in the path of development must be moved and rebuilt.
* In New Hampshire, especially beautiful or historic walls are rebuilt nearby if roadwork threatens them."

The Save-the-Wall committee made sure the village manager and the state department of transportation received copies of the article and they walked a bit taller when they discussed it in the neighborhood.

NETLIVING NOTES:

- Netliving will help obtain knowledge on a subject. I've learned to share with others as those who gave to me.
- Netliving can assist in accomplishing a tough goal. I've learned to share my defects as well as my assets with my teammates.
* Netliving can help develop a win-win situation. I've learned to become more trusting which is freedom of fear and leads to better cooperation.

CHAPTER TWENTY FOUR

TO THE TOMB

"If I were asked what is the best thing one can expect in life, I would say -- the privilege of being useful."

Eleanor Roosevelt (1884-1962)

As Roberta and Richard entered the twilight of their lives, many netliving opportunities became available. Being retired gave them the time they needed to devote to activities which interested them. They now made choices which they could not have exercised when they were working full-time.

Roberta was interested in traveling. She and her husband had set a goal of visiting all the states of the union, including Alaska and Hawaii. There was a large map mounted on a basement door covered with little markers which indicated places visited.

There was a secondary motive to their travels. Roberta had recently read that nearly one in ten of today's mature Americans move to a new state after retirement -- usually one with a milder climate. Hard on their heels are 75 million baby boomers born between 1946 and 1964 who are beginning to turn 50. Eighteen percent of 50-year-olds recently surveyed by the Del Webb Corporation, a developer of planned communities for those 55 and older, revealed plans to move when they shed their jobs. That is partly because baby boomers are better-traveled than previous generations and more likely to have moved during their careers, says Steven House, chairman of the American Association of Retirement Communities. AARC is an organization of local and state economic development people working to lure retirees to their areas.

Roberta learned that, like their predecessors, many boomers will choose to retire to places where they have vacationed. They will be tempted by shorelines, mountain peaks or balmy breezes wafting lazily over championship golf courses. They will head toward those regions that intrigued them as they passed through on business trips or the brief vacation stay. Some rely on where-to-retire books touting supposedly "the ideal locale."

To initiate the search, Roberta learned to make a list of what was important to her in retirement and a new location. The Del Webb survey found 50 year-olds look forward to managing their own time and doing the things they enjoy doing, such as travel, golf and other recreational sports. They want to take up new hobbies such as gardening, computers, needlepoint and art, and spend more time with spouse and family. More than two-thirds plan to continue working, either part-time or in a new career, while almost 70 percent plan to do volunteer work.

The most important factors in choosing a retirement site, Roberta learned, include a mild climate and low crime rate, according to a survey of subscribers to *Where to Retire* magazine. Such financial factors as reasonable housing prices, cost of living rates and low taxes also count. So do health-related aspects, such as good hospitals and the availability of continuing care retirement communities. Those surveyed also want hospitable neighbors, friends and relatives in the area. They look for good recreational facilities and an active social and cultural environment as well as adult education at a local college. They also like having a major city and an airport with commercial service nearby.

With this list in hand, Roberta and her husband narrowed the possible locations by visiting, for the second and the third time, certain favorite vacation spots and locations recommended by friends. The people with whom Roberta netlived warned against making a hasty decision, especially at planned communities which offer incentives such as free trips involving pressure sales pitches. Other retired friends who had already made the move warned that even if a place looks good after a series of shorter visits, it is one thing to visit as a tourist and quite another to live there 24 hours a day, week after week. A strong recommendation was to rent for a year before buying.

Roberta heard that retirement in a new community can be like a permanent vacation -- but only if you spend those holidays and trips getting to know whether its amenities will make you happy in the long run.

Richard and his wife, like his sister and her husband applied their netliving skills to the adventure of planning for retirement. When they entered any new situation in life, it was natural for them to seek out people who "know what is going on." Whether it was a new school, military service or a new community, they often started building an information network. As they entered retirement, they needed to netlive to get advice and counsel for all the many important decisions ahead.

This caused them to pause and review the advantages of netliving:

* While reading can provide some information, the netliving process is interactive and proactive and allows them to learn about someone's personal experience (such as living in a condo, moving to Florida or selecting a financial planner).
* It provides a variety of perspectives from other's successes as well as mistakes in similar situations.
* Netliving conversations allow for probing, asking follow-up questions and understanding the true feelings of those providing the information Richard and Roberta both knew why netliving works as a method of gathering information, obtaining introductions, doing research or building a support group. Netliving is a superior technique for several reasons:
* People generally feel great satisfaction from helping others and giving advice. Asking someone for help is a form of recognition.
* In most netliving situations, there is at least an implied contract to return the favor, to assist the person in the future with their needs.
* For most people, meeting new people is interesting and fun. Netliving is simple, Roberta and Richard pointed out to their respective spouses. It is something they had always used but may not have always realized its full potential as a process for obtaining information,

introductions and assistance. They looked at the steps to effective netliving:

* Develop a netliving list. Initially don't attempt to qualify the list (similar to brainstorming). Try to recall as many names as you can; include relatives, friends, co-workers, superiors, subordinates, classmates, business associates, clergy, neighbors, etc.
* Prioritize the list around different retirement issues which require information, advice or introductions. Consider issues such as financial investments, living in adult communities, returning to school, volunteering, part-time work, moving to a different part of the country, consulting and others.
* Arrange an in-person appointment if at all possible. While phone contact, e-mail or regular mail can sometimes work, a personal visit is far more effective.
* Establish rapport by providing background information about yourself and any decisions you are about to make. It is important the person you are netliving with has this background in order to put advice in the context of your personal situation. It also adds to your credibility.
* Involve your contacts in your situation. Ask probing questions regarding their experience, decisions or sources of information.
* Seek introductions to others who might serve as additional resources on issues related to your retirement. Seek to build as large a network as possible so that you can turn to it in the future.
* Offer yourself as a resource for their future needs or those of their family and friends.

Richard offered two examples of the netliving process to his wife, Patricia and his brother-in-law, James.

TELEPHONE CONTACT:
Jackie dialed Mike's phone number. Mike answered, "Hello?" Jackie said, "Hello Mike, this is Jackie Brown. You may not remember me, but I was in Systems Engineering in

Washington D.C. when you were Branch Manager." "Oh yes. It's been a few years. How are you?' he replied. "I'm fine, " she replied, "I'm glad you remember. The reason I called you is I am planning an early retirement soon, and in talking with some IBMers they mentioned your name as someone who could help. I am considering buying a condo in Hilton Head and I could use your input since I understand you bought one there some years ago," she continued.

Mike said, "That's right. We generally have had a good experience." Jackie continued, "I'm going to be down there in about two weeks looking around. I was wondering if you would have some time to spend with me?" "Sure. What are the Dates?" Mike replied.

PERSONAL CONTACT:
Mike said, "Hi Jackie, It's good to see you again. You haven't changed much. Come in." Jackie said, "Good to see you Mike. Retirement has been good to you I see." Mike replied, "I'm not complaining, although sometimes I miss the challenge of work." Jackie continued, "First let me bring you up to date. After you left Washington, I was put in charge of supporting systems designs for a Department of Defense project that went very well. Last year, I was transferred back to New Jersey. It's been great, but I'm really beginning to think about taking it easy. Retirement is beginning to look real good to me."

"That's just great," Mike replied, "I had kind of lost track of you. As you may know, I took off early a few years ago. How can I help you?" "How much time do we have?" she asked, "so I can keep this from being an all-day reunion." "I'm good for about two hours before I tee off at the club" He replied. "Good," she continued, "my initial planning centers around where I'm going to live. Since I think that will dictate a lot of the other aspects of retirement, I have looked at Florida and California, but now I'm beginning to focus on some other areas.

"Sounds like you're researching it very well," Mike said. "We found that it's vital to talk with as many people as possible to make a good decision." He continued. "Tell me Mike, What were the reasons you finally chose Hilton Head? She asked.

"Well, first we liked the climate," He began. "We like to be near the ocean and the many golf courses that located here." He continued. "All in all it has turned out to be just the right location for us." He concluded. "So that part has worked out well?" Jackie asked. "Yes, in fact one point I didn't mention was the nice people we have met down here." Mike continued.

"How are the resale values if for some reason I don't like it?" she asked. "I've seen some numbers on Hilton Head; what's your experience?" she continued. "Do you know anyone who has sold? she concluded. Mike replied, "That's important right now, because recently there has been a real change in market value that hasn't been reflected in the numbers I've seen." "My view is that we are in a tight economy and once things loosen up the prices will return to normal." He replied. "So you don't buy there general view?" she asked. "Right. Several of our friends have sold recently to move elsewhere. Their experience was positive," He said. "They received within 5% of their asking price. You can't expect to do much better than that in this kind of economy." he continued.

"One of my interests will be to return to school. I'm thinking of an art program." she said. "I've always painted as a hobby but I've had little formal training." she continued. "That wasn't one of my interests when I retired, so I'm not sure I can help on that." He responded. "Do you know of anyone who has pursued school down here?" She continued. He replied, "If I remember correctly, Mary O'Brien, one of the women in our bridge club, took some courses a few years ago. Why don't I give you her number? Tell her I told you to call."

Jackie said, "One of my alternative locations is the Hatteras areas of North Carolina." "Did you look there?" she asked. "No, we didn't, although I've heard some good things about that area," he replied. "Do you know anyone who did?" she continued. "Not that I can remember. But I'll ask around at the club today. I'm sure that I'll come across someone who did." he replied. "If you do, please put them in touch with me. Let me give you may phone number and address. Mike, you have been so helpful. I can't thank you enough. Let's stay in touch." She concluded. Mike said, "I wish we had more time. In the next few weeks. I'll send you some information we collected that might help you."

∞∞∞∞∞∞∞∞∞∞∞∞∞∞∞∞∞∞∞∞∞∞∞∞∞∞∞∞∞∞∞∞∞∞∞∞∞

Richard asked, "How did Jackie do?" Look at the techniques of netliving. Did she miss anything? What about her active listening? Obviously, this example was an easy one. Others can be more difficult. There will be situations where the contact won't have the necessary information; situations where gaining introductions to others with the data will be the true goal.

During a difficult winter of the mid nineteen nineties, Roberta, Richard and their spouses decided to become "snow birds" the following winter. They had completed their netliving and had zeroed in on the Atlantic coast of Florida since they all loved the ocean and wanted to be on the beach.

All summer long they were busy as beavers getting ready for their winter away from home. They planned to leave on January first, since on New Years Day there aren't many big trucks on the road. They would stop over in North Carolina to break the trip.

Richard, the practical one, had been doing some netliving among his older friends and the subject of "getting your house in order" came up; such issues as living wills, the right to die, DNR (do not resuscitate), medical power of attorney, etc. He listened and then shared what he had learned with his spouse and Roberta and her spouse.

These issues brought with them strong emotional feelings, but they were important to address. The four friends believed they should be taken care of before they traveled south. They consulted an attorney who was recommended through netliving. Earlier, they had also purchased grave sites through a special veterans' offering in a memorial garden.

On New Years Day they left their northern homes to follow the sun to Florida in their shiny new mini-van. It was an exciting day for the four of them They were looking forward to the adventure.

Upon arriving at their rental condo, they were treated to a breathtaking view of the Atlantic Ocean. Richard was reminded of being on the bridge of an old gray navy ship like those he had sailed while in the Navy. He could see for miles out to sea.

Roberta pointed out that if you looked out from the kitchen window you would see the Intercoastal waterway. It was an ideal location for spending the winter. The people in this eight story high-rise apartment building were friendly. Most of them were in the same boat. The had not been away from their loved ones before for any length of time, so the experience drew them to each other.

The middle-aged couple who managed the building were friendly and helpful. They pointed out places to shop and locations of restaurants where one could find a good meal at a reasonable price. They held a meeting for all the "snow birds" as they affectionately called the northerners who were escaping winter's blast. During the meeting, long-time renters took leadership roles and planned activities for the next three months.

After the meeting, the netliving continued. Richard was interested in finding golfing and tennis partners. Roberta was interested in the water aerobic class that had been mentioned. Richard's spouse was a dedicated shopper, so she wanted to know the location of shopping malls. Roberta's husband was an auto and aviation buff so he was interested in the auto racing circuit as well as the aviation museums.

The foursome were always on the go. They formed great friendships and had three wonderful months in the sun, walking the beach every morning at sun-up, diligently searching the beach for treasures in the form of keepsake sea shells as they enjoyed the extreme leisure of being away from it all.

There were spring training baseball games to attend and side trips to visit the Everglades where Richard was able to video live alligators with his new camcorder. They had an opportunity to see "sea cows" in the warm water of an inland river. These manatees seemed longer and thinner in the water than any picture Roberta had ever seen.

As the month of April approached, they gathered their belongings and began packing the mini-van for the two-day trip north on Interstate 95 to the homes and families awaiting their return.

Richard was behind the wheel when they pulled out from the entrance ramp onto the interstate. Suddenly an eighteen-wheeler came out of nowhere and crushed the mini-van. The sound of metal-on-metal was deafening. The mini-van was smashed from the rear and pushed down interstate # 95 for two hundred feet. When the pile of rubble that once was their vehicle came to a stop there were loud shouts of pain. Roberta and her husband, James, who were sitting in the back seat were killed instantly. Richard's wife Patricia was in critical condition on the passenger side of the mini-van which had no airbag. Richard was the fortunate one to have an airbag and it saved his life.

He was unconscious when the first travelers came to administer first aid. One young nurse who was on her way home from work determined that three of the four occupants were dead on the scene. Her main concern was keeping Richard alive until the rescue squad arrived. She kept him quiet and kept telling him in soothing terms that ,"Everything was going to be all right." The EMC team arrived in about seven minutes, but to the off-duty nurse it seemed much longer than that.

They stabilized Richard and put him on a gurney and placed him in the ambulance.

He was semi-conscious when they drove away from the scene so they were encouraged. They took him to the closest hospital which was located at Daytona Beach. The hospital admitting personnel contacted his three adult children and they in turn notified the building managers where they had stayed all winter.

When the word spread throughout their building, The Silver Wings, there was much grief and everyone asked what they could do to help. Bill, the building manager took one of the tenants who knew Richard and drove over to the hospital to visit him and see if they could help with any of the funeral arrangements for the other three unfortunate "snow birds."

Richard and Roberta's children arrived at the Daytona Beach Airport within hours of receiving the alarming phone call. All six of them were in a state of shock and had no idea what to do next. This is where Bill's calm approach he learned in the military paid off. He gently made suggestions as to how they could proceed and through his contacts in the area was able to netlive to determine the proper procedure to transport the bodies to their northern destination.

This was a trying time for all the young people, but especially Roberta's since they lost both parents in one fell swoop. Richard was recovering quite well although he had some serious bruises. Fortunately he had no broken bones or serious cuts. Most of the damaged had been caused by the airbag exploding. He was a comfort to his children and his niece and nephews. Bill had them come and stay temporally in the building where their parents had spent such a joyful three months. The remaining residents baked them cookies and some other comfort food to do what little they could to ease some the pain.

The funeral was delayed for several weeks while Richard recovered sufficiently to fly back home to take care of the final arrangements for the wake and burial. As the weeks passed and the funerals became history, Richard was left with the sad memory of the fatal crash. Through netliving with the funeral director he was able to obtain a grief counseling program for his three children along with his niece, two nephews and himself.

This was a powerful program conducted by the funeral director's wife who had been a classmate of Roberta in college. At the last session of the grief coping program the group was encouraged to continue meeting to netlive with each other as a support group for at least a year.

The young people felt this was not necessary because they had such busy schedules and they wanted to get on with their lives. Richard felt differently and continued to go to the meetings every week. He met other men and women in the support group who had similar stories to tell of the loss they felt and especially one widow who had lost her husband in an auto accident similar to the one Richard had experienced.

In a few months like many other problems in life he began to feel less and less sad and one day at a time he realized that it was important he get on with his life. He was a pillar of strength for not only his own children but his niece and nephews.

Richard found his spiritual life helped him pass through this valley of tears. He knew that some day he would be reunited with his wife, sister and brother-in-law. This helped his grief considerably. There was hope and something to look forward to in the hereafter.

The widow who had lost her husband in the tragic auto accident was helpful to Richard because they had much in common and could buoy each other up when the other was feeling sad. She was a petite lady barely five feet tall with an upbeat and outgoing personality. She had children about the same ages as Richard's and they discussed situations as they came up and helped each other with family decisions.

Richard became active in a volunteer program for the blind known as "Books on Tape" where he read the classics into a microphone and his well-modulated, articulate baritone voice was recorded for the listening pleasure of the sight impaired. Based on this initial success he was asked to read the entire Wall Street Journal live on a special radio station serving the blind every Monday morning at 9:00 a.m.

This volunteering was encouraged by Ann, his widow friend for she experienced a feeling of relief herself for her grief by giving service to others. They decided to volunteer together to serve meals to the homeless once a month at Saint Patrick's church in the inner city. They enjoyed the fellowship of the other volunteers and the gratitude of those they served.

This volunteering exposed Richard to another person who was active in the RSVP program. The Retired Senior Volunteer Program has many facets to it but the one that appealed to Richard was an acting program. He had always wanted to appear on stage and show his talents to the world. Here was his golden opportunity.

This thespian program entailed writing a one-act play and appearing on stage to act out what he had written. The audience was usually patients in a veteran's hospital or homes for the aged. The reward he received for this effort was witnessed in the appreciative audience who mouthed the words of his songs along with he and the other performers.

Richard found himself so busy with his volunteering and his caring for the rest of his family that he had little time to feel sorry for himself.

NETLIVING NOTES:

* Netliving will help you obtain life planning information. I've learned that you should always leave loved ones with loving words. It may be the last time you see them.
* Netliving will expand your knowledge of living. I've learned that it's not what happens to people that's important. It's what they do about it.
* Netliving will assist you in preparing for your final days. I've learned that either you control your attitude or it controls you.

About the Author

John C. "Jack" Durkin, a human resource executive for more than thirty-five years, has successfully utilized netliving principles to fill job openings and obtain critical benchmark data. During this time period he faciliated dozens of workshops for his employer and others.

The "Alumni Career Network" at alma mater was developed and chaired by him. He also chaired "New Careers for Older Americans" the function of which was to find positions for displaced older workers using the netliving approach.

A navy veteran, he holds a BS from John Carroll and an MBA from Kent State. JCU, where he taught human resource, awarded him its highest honor, the Alumni Medal. He was voted outstanding member of the the Cleveland Chapter of the Society for Human Resource Management. Currently, he operates a successful consulting business.

www.ingramcontent.com/pod-product-compliance
Lightning Source LLC
Chambersburg PA
CBHW020734180526
45163CB00001B/238